Constructing Suburbs

Cities and Regions
Planning, Policy and Management

A series edited by Seymour J. Mandelbaum
University of Pennsylvania, Philadelphia

This book is part of a series. The publisher will accept continuation orders which may be cancelled at any time and which provide for automatic billing and shipping of each title in the series upon publication. Please write for details.

Constructing Suburbs

Competing Voices in a Debate Over Urban Growth

Ann Forsyth

University of Massachusetts, Amherst
USA

Taylor & Francis

Taylor & Francis Group

LONDON AND NEW YORK

First published 1999
by Gordon and Breach Publishers.
Reprinted 2004
by Taylor & Francis,
11 New Fetter Lane, London EC4P 4EE

Transferred to Digital Printing 2004

Copyright © 1999 OPA (Overseas Publishers Association) N.V. Published
by license under the Gordon and Breach Publishers imprint.

British Library Cataloguing in Publication Data

Forsyth, Ann
   Constructing suburbs : competing voices in a debate over
   urban growth. – (Cities and regions : planning, policy and
   management ; v. 2 – ISSN 1027-1007)
   1. Urbanization 2. City planning
   I. Title
   307.7'6

ISBN 90-5700-527-1

Contents

Illustrations

Figures

Tables

Introduction to the Series

Cities and Regions: Planning, Policy and Management is an international series of case studies addressed to students in programs leading to professional careers in urban and regional affairs and to established practitioners of the complex crafts of planning, policy analysis and public management. The series will focus on the work-worlds of the practitioners and the ways in which the construction of narratives shapes the course of events and our understanding of them. The international character of the series is intended to help both novice and experienced professionals extend their terms of reference, learning from "strangers" in unfamiliar settings.

Seymour J. Mandelbaum

Acknowledgments

This book took its toll on many people. Although I promised not to name them in my writing, without the generosity of the people I interviewed and observed this study would not have been possible.

In the United States, Seymour Mandelbaum reviewed an article from this project and gave continued support and detailed advice in his role of series editor. Dolores Hayden also gave tremendous encouragement. The study owes its genesis to Peter Marris, whose work has shaped the way I make sense of cities. This book started out as a dissertation and committee members John Forester, Susan Christopherson, and Carol Greenhouse each contributed to its development.

In Australia, the Department of Architecture at the University of Sydney granted me an affiliation during my main fieldwork year (1991–1992). I would like to thank Colin James who arranged my affiliation, Elizabeth Boesel who shared her knowledge about western Sydney, and Anna Rubbo who made me feel welcome. Ellen Forsyth lived through the difficulties of fieldwork with me and lent me her car to go to places trains and buses did not. Richard Cardew at Macquarie University helped me clarify my questions and organized my eight-month stay in Sydney in 1995. Conversations with Patrick Troy, after an article from the work had won the Peter Harrison Prize, helped me rethink some key issues. Ian Burnley, Sharon Fingland, Simon Fox, Geoff King, Martin Payne, Glen Searle, and the staff at the Western Sydney Regional Organisation of Councils gave me valuable advice or assistance at crucial times.

Several other people provided support during the writing process. Peter Marris and Seymour Mandelbaum each read the work twice and helped tremendously in clarifying my argument. Doug

Albertson and Carlos Balsas also read drafts; and Lisa Stallworth read significant sections. Leonie Sandercock, Wendy Sarkissian, Gwen Urey, and Francie Viggiani gave intellectual and personal support, often in the face of quite complex geographies. John Friedmann, Dana Harp, Rob Hodder, Rebecca Hovey, Karen Jones, Laurie Langlois De Perno, Mark Lapping, Bob Letcher, Amy Lind, Will Mallet, Wendy McFarren, Fred Rose, Paul Schimek, Daphne Spain, Drury Tallant, Jim Thogmorton, and Rick Troiano gave advice or practical help in question formulation, research, and writing.

Scholarships from the Victorian and South Australian branches of the Australian Federation of University Women, and a summer grant from the Department of City and Regional Planning at Cornell, provided financial support for my dissertation research. An International Fellowship from the American Association of University Women supported the dissertation writing.

Three chapters of this book appeared in part elsewhere. Thanks to the *Journal of the American Planning Association* (**63**, 1: 45–60) for permission to reprint portions of chapter two, originally published in 1997 as "Five Images of a Suburb: Perspectives on a New Urban Development." The *Journal of Architectural and Planning Research* granted permission to reprint much of chapter three, forthcoming as "Soundbite Cities: Imagining Futures in Debates over Urban Form." The *Journal of Urban Affairs* (**17**, 3: 241–262) in 1995 published an earlier version of chapter five as "Privatization: Infrastructure on the Urban Edge." It appears here with their permission. The New South Wales Department of Urban Affairs and Planning generously gave permission to reproduce Figures 2, 5, and 8.

Finally, thanks to my editor Kirsty Mackay, who answered all my queries with good humor.

Introduction

In 1991 I went to Sydney, Australia, thinking that I was going to study a large suburban development project in its transition from planning to implementation. If the project – Rouse Hill – had gone according to schedule, this volume would have tracked adjustments in the "best laid plans" when development finance is arranged, roads and pipes are put in place, and the first residents move into their new homes.

In fact, the project had already fallen behind schedule before I arrived and its future was uncertain. A national debate about the course of urban developments centered on Australia's ability to sustain its familiar patterns of settlement. In Sydney – a metropolitan area home to over one fifth of Australia's population – that debate brought planning for some large suburban projects to a halt. Rouse Hill survived the controversy; when I returned to Australia in 1995 around a thousand of its lots had been sold. However, the first bulldozers had hardly begun to work when policy makers announced limitations on the scheme (Department of Planning [DoP] 1995). In the short-term the development will go ahead, although the target population has been scaled back to about a third of its earlier projection of 250,000. In the long-term more of the area may be developed, but this is likely to be a difficult and controversial process.

In this context I reconceived the research. What emerged was a study of the ways in which several fundamentally different accounts of the world shaped the planning of the project and the working lives of the planners, development professionals, and activists who were involved in the development. The case study also became a way of examining how these groups approached urban development at a time when its context was changing rapidly. By examining a large project over a number of years, I was also able to analyze how ideas about urban form changed over time and how the shifting ways of imagining and debating urban development interacted with the power of money, political connections, and bureaucratic control to reshape physical development.

The accounts I listened to were all ways of reconciling a large number of social, economic, and environmental needs into a plan of action. All were justified by proponents as in some sense representing a public interest in terms of various economic, social, and environmental goals. In the Rouse Hill project, professionals and activists frequently claimed to be creating a holistic or balanced position, telling the whole story, or providing a rational outcome.[1] That one's view on urban form was more comprehensive or rational seemed to matter, and few people expressed doubts that they had found the most comprehensive and rational view. However, these views were not commensurable; they were not based on a common set of priorities and values.

On one level this language was not so surprising as planners have long been concerned that their work is comprehensive, rational in process or in outcomes, and serves a wider public good. Even those critical of mainstream planning have often been critical of its lack of these characteristics; for example, wanting planning to be more inclusive of less powerful groups, that is to be more comprehensive. On another level, however, it was intriguing that a similar language of rationality and balance was used to articulate very different perspectives on urban growth.

This is the broader context of the study, although the particular case of Rouse Hill focused the research on a specific set of issues. The rhetoric of planning in Australia, during the past decade, was confronted with a dilemma. The ideal of a home-owning egalitarian democracy came up against new financial and environmental constraints as development became more expensive and ecological issues more pressing. Various groups proposed different ways of reinterpreting the public interest in the face of the dilemma. Some environmentalists introduced a fundamentally new conception of the public interest that emphasized basic ecological principles of survival; property developers, and planners favoring expansion, tried to adapt a traditional egalitarian and pro-growth framework to new circumstances; others favored limiting growth by consolidating urban areas, trying to create a compromise between environmental concerns and housing needs. Each position had obvious strengths and weaknesses. The pro-growth group could not solve the environmental problems except at great expense and with quite a lot of uncertainty as to whether problems were actually solved. The environmentalists did not have a ready resolution of housing needs. Those supporting consolidation faced the objection that the new higher-density housing they proposed would be less desirable than the traditional suburban home. Each side used images of good and bad cities to bolster their vision. Each side fought over the formal planning process and the process of infrastructure finance and development as a way of obtaining their goals.

By the 1990s these somewhat abstract positions were articulated in terms of a fairly limited set of actual policy alternatives for urban growth. Some choices for changing growth patterns had already been rejected in the 1980s as major options, although they had not entirely disappeared from the political agenda. These included stopping immigration, and decentralizing growth to new towns or existing smaller cities.[2] This left two real choices in the early 1990s. The first was to continue suburban expansion, and find a way to finance the cost of infrastructure and environmental control in developments such as Rouse Hill. The second involved consolidating existing settlements. In the short- and medium-term, the first of these options won. The financial obstacles were overcome by the device of privatization, although as property developers assumed more of the cost of infrastructure development the housing became more expensive and expansion lost some of its justification as an instrument of the egalitarian suburban ideal. The property developers also did not assume any of the cost of new social infrastructure, such as schools, so reluctant government departments and non-profits were left to do that, leading some to question the quality of social life in new areas. The outcome, then, was hard to justify in terms of the public interest, as those supporting urban expansion first represented that interest, and harder still to justify in terms of other conceptions of the public interest.

The arguments for consolidation were more robustly taken up in the 1995 metropolitan plan. This document projected slower growth than the previous metropolitan plan, published in 1988. The 1995 plan also proposed that only about one third of the 520,000 units needed in Sydney, as the population increases from its 1991 figure of 3.7 million to 4.5 million in 2021, will be on the fringe, rather than a majority of them (DoP 1995, 75; DoP 1988). This was the plan that also scaled back Rouse Hill.

In the case of Rouse Hill's first stage, however, the momentum of prior commitments gave an edge to those supporting its development. The idea of expansion had been endorsed in principle in decades before environmental concerns had grown prominent. Public and private sector developers who already owned land in the area had a good deal at stake, and could wait out the opposition. It would have taken sustained, insistent, and powerful opposition to prevent all development, and that was not forthcoming. Why not? There seems to have been, at least until the end of the 1980s when the major decisions were being made, no serious alternative to expansion. Some critics did complain about the costs of development and warned about environmental problems. However, they did not succeed in creating an alternative image of a good city that was comfortable for Australians. This lack of a strong alternative urban vision meant that the momentum of real estate development faced opposition that only became powerful in the early 1990s, too late to totally stop the project.

The environmental, economic, and social issues that people fought over in Rouse Hill parallel those dealt with in recent intellectual arguments about sustainability, pluralism, privatization, economic power, and justice. It is no mistake that these issues were the focus, as throughout the 1990s these have been major concerns in many planning processes in many parts of the world. [3] They are also likely to continue to be key areas of concern in the coming decades as urban development projects are pushed into ever more difficult sites. In this international context, the Australian case is interesting in that it stakes out a middle ground between the planning and urban development situations in the more developer-driven context of the United States and the more government-led and centralized Great Britain. This middle ground is reinforced by Australian planners' tendencies to adopt planning ideas from these two countries. [4]

Context

Four areas of scholarly work offered ways to approach these questions and issues. Writing on the public interest gave insights for examining competing claims to balance, rational, and holistic approaches. Work analyzing conflict though an interpretive rather than an interest-based framework seemed to offer ways of understanding conflicts between people and groups with ostensibly the same interests. Research on narrative and discourse analysis, popular in planning from the 1980s, had the potential to be extended beyond studies of individual plans and planners, or short planning episodes. Finally, discussions in anthropology about how to represent complex societies provided models for dealing with the authorial problem of preserving some of that complexity in "writing culture."

The public interest can be defined as those interests that people have in common as members of the public (Barry 1965, 190); something is in the public interest if it "serves the ends of the whole public" rather than just a sector of it (Meyerson and Banfield 1955, 322).[5] Within this definition there is room for a number of different ways of arriving at an understanding of what people have in common; for some it is a process of balancing up different individual interests or ideas about the public interest, for others it means tapping into a set of common ends (Meyerson and Banfield 1955, 323–325; Howe 1994, 77–78). The exact content of the public interest in planning has never been completely clear either, and emphases on aesthetics, efficiency, individual interests, hygiene, equity, community, and ecology have existed in different balances at different times.

In dealing with this issue of the public interest, planners are concerned about the roles of powerful groups like real estate and industrial capitalists, or political elites. These groups often argue that their private interests and the public interest coincide, however that is not always clearly the case. In addition, planners are confronted with a growing number of popular social movements – like environmentalisms, women's movements, ethnic and national groups, and anti-government movements – groups that also claim to represent a public interest, even if in some cases there are multiple publics.

However, to say that some concept like the public interest is a crucial concept in planning does not imply that anyone can agree what it is or can measure it. That is why the words used by planners – the rhetorical devices and arguments, the everyday discourses – are so important.[6] Planners not only seek to analyze the important issues and needs that must be dealt with to satisfy the public interest, but in doing so planners also define what the public interest is. Planners' arguments are both technical and moral.

In examining this debate I brought to the study a set of ideas coming out of research that had explored the politics of urban development not only as an example of competing interests but also in terms of differing interpretations of those interests. Through the case of Rouse Hill I came to see that suburban development involved the working out of quite complex ideas about nature and equality, family and opportunity, insiders and outsiders. This working out was accomplished in public debates and influenced governments, property developers, and other professionals. Although the debates were certainly informed and constrained by people's economic interests, roles, and social positions, they were more complex and interesting than mere reflections of mainly economic characteristics, involving different interpretations of this wider context (Fainstein 1994; Logan and Molotch 1987; Mansbridge 1990; Perin 1977; Sandercock 1990, 266; Schwarz and Thompson 1990).[7]

In the 1980s and early 1990s there had also been a great deal of work exposing the rhetorical nature of planning and related disciplines, and the political nature of planning communication and discourse.[8] This third area of work intrigued me, but generally dealt with relatively bounded planning projects and events rather than large developments like Rouse Hill. It frequently examined individual documents, interviews, or short-term interactions such as meetings, and had little to say about the influence of those rhetorical and communicative practices on planning outcomes. I worried that without a larger context it was hard to judge the effects of positions and views and it seemed that the influence of planning arguments on planning outcomes was worth examining. Other work on language and planning did deal with general and long-running debates over planning; however, this lost some of the useful detail provided by case studies (Beauregard 1993; Dear 1989; Marcuse 1989; Smith 1996).

In 1991, as I started this research, I thought that a case study of a large and long-running development, including interviews with people from different sides of the controversy, offered the chance to assess some of the effects of positions and rhetorical strategies. It also made it possible to go beyond analyzing how people represented themselves and their agencies, to examine how they were perceived by others as well. With this kind of extended study I thought it would be possible to build up a more complex picture of the rhetorical, cultural, political, and economic aspects of contemporary development practices (see also Grant 1994; Hillier 1993; Marris 1987; Peattie 1987; Rabinow 1989).

The influence these planning debates had on the planning process, and the urban development itself, required an analysis of power relations. In this study I came to define power fairly simply following Giddens, where: "power relations in social systems are regularized relations of autonomy and dependence. Power relations are always two-way; that is to say however subordinate an actor may be in a social relationship the very fact of involvement in that relationship gives him or her a certain amount of power over the other" (Giddens 1979, 6). That is, rather than seeing power as something held by a few I was interested in the "manifold relations of power" (Foucault 1980, 93) evident in the project with various actors trying to gain control of the situation in order to act in the way they thought best. Power also operated through a variety of mechanisms with different persons and groups having access to different forms of power in different areas: economic, political, administrative, and in the realm of ideas.[9]

My particular emphasis on the power of ideas may seem unusual as other forms of power are more commonly associated with urban development. As a number of other authors have pointed out, however, ideas had power as persuasion, inspiration, legitimation, rationalization, and as a means of identity formation (Gottdiener 1977, 117; Throgmorton 1996; Nelson et al. 1987). Some groups skillfully presented their ideas in ways that they expected to be compelling and in fact had an influence on the project.

In this study I focused on middle-level, middle-class professionals and activists. These people were the technical and intellectual workers who shaped the week-to-week running of the project: planners, environmental bureaucrats, staff of regional and international environmental groups, and resident leaders. These types of people had frequently been the subject of study in earlier work on planning rhetoric. To one side of these professionals and activists were the government and business elites who had considerable autonomy due to their ability to finance infrastructure and their influence in state parliamentary cabinet. They were not, however, all-powerful. For example, in developing their land in a timely and thus profitable manner, those involved in property development depended on the cooperation of others such as the professional planners I studied. Unorganized local residents similarly focused much of their energy on this middle-level group both in terms of getting access to information and expressing opposition. For example, at a time of intense pressure on the local governments by the directors of the Rouse Hill Infrastructure Consortium that needed rezonings to secure loans, Baulkham Hills Council received almost 1000 written objections to their Draft Local Environmental Plan (Baulkham Hills Shire Council 1991). The time needed to read and respond to these submissions made speedy planning difficult. This ultimately was an example of the economic and political power of the consortium, that had contacts in state cabinet, being resisted by the landowning public. However, it was some of the professionals I studied who were in the middle, reading all those letters and writing replies, engaging in communicative and rhetorical actions.

Finally, in terms of scholarly work that influenced me, in the 1980s and 1990s anthropologists had been exploring issues of "multivocality" as a critique of much previous anthropological writing. This earlier writing had suppressed differences among those being studied, often by drawing the boundaries of study very tightly in time, space, and social grouping. It had also tended to drown out all voices except that of the anthropologist (Clifford 1988a; Mascia-Lees *et al.* 1989). Of course this was not true of all classics in anthropology, but these critiques of previous, seamless, writing offered a useful way of dealing with research and writing about situations of conflict. Work in the anthropology of law and disputes offered a number of prototypes (e.g. Clifford 1988b; Engel 1984; Krasniewicz 1992; Sarat and Felstiner 1986).

Of course the people I studied were not the marginalized colonial and postcolonial subjects of such concern to anthropologists, and in fact most of them were busy producing their own "texts." They are also an audience for this text in a way unlike that traditionally envisaged in anthropological work. However, these debates about giving voice to subjects of study, and about writing style, were still relevant in that they dealt with the issue I faced; that of representing a situation with many voices.

Responding to this body of work, I have constructed an account of Rouse Hill from four different angles. In chapters one and four, the volume explores how the formal planning process created a "Development Area" out of a location. In chapter two, it analyzes five perspectives on urban form that confronted each other as the development was about to start. In chapter three, it examines how the project's future was represented as if it would become another city – a Los Angeles, Toronto, or Canberra – and then judged by their problems and strengths. In chapter five, it outlines how partial privatization allowed public and private developers to keep the project moving forward. Through the four narratives I show that there were multiple ways of experiencing and interpreting the project. In the end it was not possible to say the "real" story revolved around the formal planning process, or economic power, or who was most adept at framing the planning debates. All these were important at different times, for different groups, and in different parts of the development.

Methods

In examining these issues of planning ideas and actions I looked at the day-to-day work of a set of professionals and activists; the writing, reading, drawing, talking, and keeping silent that form the repertoire of what planners and activists do. Most of the research for this study was done between July 1991 and July 1992 in Sydney, the largest of Australia's cities. I also returned in 1995. The first half of the 1990s was an exciting time to be looking at planning issues as the public and professional interest in urban sprawl was on an upswing. This was an important issue given Australia's high level of urbanization. In 1991, 85 percent of its population was classed as urban and three-fifths lived in just five cities of a million or more: Sydney, Melbourne, Brisbane, Perth, and Adelaide (McLennan 1996, 80). Numerous state and federal government initiatives dealt with questions about future patterns of urban growth. One informant suggested this rise in interest was a reaction to rising "community awareness" and was following a US trend: "I mean all these social phenomena, they appear in the States and two weeks later they appear in Sydney" (Claude, interview). This comment had some truth for me personally as it had been my

experiences in US cities, particularly Los Angeles, that had provoked my interest in the character of the growth debate in Sydney.
Over the main year of research Rouse Hill, and the major actors
involved in its development, were frequently in the news. Two
independent inquiries into the Department of Housing recommended abolishing or dramatically restructuring it because of
mismanagement (Gyles 1992; Mant 1992). In the Australian
political system local governments have relatively few powers and
are subject to a high level of state government control. In this period
Baulkham Hills Shire Council, one of the local government areas
the Rouse Hill Development Area was located in, also underwent
external inquiries nearly having its local planning powers taken
away by the state government (Cook 1991a).

These events both helped and hindered my research. While I
was able to attend public meetings on Rouse Hill and on issues
of metropolitan growth, the heated debates made gaining access
to sensitive data more difficult. I was also working in the aftermath
of Sharon Beder who, as a doctoral student researching engineering decisions on sewage treatment, inadvertently discovered
that the Water Board and State Pollution Control Commission
had not released the results of studies showing extraordinarily
high concentrations of pollutants in Sydney ocean fish (Beder
1989, 112–114). Leaked to the press, this information caused a
major controversy. Several of my interviewees asked me if I was
trying to "do a Sharon Beder" and expose secrets. For some I
think this possibility increased frankness; but for others it had
the opposite effect. This was a particular issue for the Department
of Housing that was under investigation as part of a Royal
Commission (Gyles 1992). Given these difficulties, the advantage
of including interviews and observations in the research design
was in being able to gain answers to a somewhat different set of
questions than those being answered in public documents,
conferences, and media reports. With a focus on multiple groups,
and multiple processes within the development, I was also
sensitive to people's silences as well as their talk.

My data include 38 formal interviews with at least a two
representatives of all major organizations involved with the
development. I conducted these in 1991 and 1992. I attended over
40 formal meetings about Rouse Hill or about growth more

generally, conducted dozens of informal interviews, and had conversations with the people I came to know through this process.[10] I observed the operations of two regional organizations. I also reviewed hundreds of documents: planning reports; activist publications; newspaper, radio, and television reports; parliamentary and corporate records; and an architectural competition for the case study site. Only those documents I directly cite are listed in the reference list.[11] I visited the site, and by 1995 I was able to see the new sewage treatment plant along with hundreds of new houses.

I asked formal interviewees for a history of their involvement in Rouse Hill; what they thought were the main issues in the development; why they thought other people saw things differently; where they saw Sydney being in twenty or thirty years time; key experiences that had shaped their own ideas about urban development; and why they thought people lived in cities. A few individuals did not allow me to tape their interviews but most did not object. Whether migrants or native-born, involved professionally or as activists, interviewees were quite articulate and homogenous; almost all had university degrees and middle-class jobs.

Although Rouse Hill as a project was too large to hide, I promised anonymity to those I interviewed. Quotations from transcripts are cited with a pseudonym.[12] Toward this same purpose, meetings that were not completely public are cited as "Meeting X" where X indicates a location in my fieldnotes and names are, again, pseudonyms.

My promise of anonymity means that at times I have had to change or omit small parts of transcripts in order to protect identities. Unlike authors interviewing individuals without reference to specific named projects, I have also had to minimize reference to some personal attributes of my informants. To create more elaborate profiles of participants would have undermined my promise of anonymity.

Apart from these changes I have only lightly edited transcripts seeking to enable other interpretations of these data. I took out some idiosyncratically repetitious phrases like "you know" or "sort of" but left in other potentially distracting phrases where informants circled around the subject (see also Perin 1977, 15). Where the quotations were responding to one of my questions I have included the question. However, often one question led to a rather lengthy and free-ranging discussion – professionals and activists are often quite talkative – and many quotes are taken from the midst of these long passages.

Where people I interviewed spoke in public situations, or produced written work where they claimed authorship, I have followed normal academic practice and attributed their comments. A few times in this study the same person is quoted using a pseudonym from an interview; using their real name where they claim authorship; and in cases where they have written reports representing a group, as an organization. These different settings are reflected in the way personal names are used in this text. Pseudonyms used in the interview transcripts are all first names; published authors are indicated with their last names only. Only public personalities involved in the Sydney or national scene are referred to using both first and second names.

Given my focus on the public face of the debate, all the documents I used were publicly available although the definition of *public* deserves some comment. Many of the documents I used were published and widely distributed. Many of the conferences I attended were inexpensive and well advertised. Government inquiries assembled a wide range of very interesting submissions that were often available for the price of the photocopies. These were obviously part of a public debate. A second level of documents and meetings was very important but not quite as obviously public. Minutes of meetings in interdepartmental government working groups, particularly those held in the early 1980s, were widely circulated and thus available from a fair number of key players. Many reports with limited circulation, even ones that were initially confidential, were eventually placed in organizational libraries. These were often leaked before making it onto those library shelves. Background material produced by the state government was also available through the Freedom of Information Act; although as many documents were circulating as photocopies, or placed in public files held by community groups, I was able to avoid this formality.

As someone trained in physical and social planning, and with a keen lay interest in environmental issues, I was very similar to many of the professionals and activists I interviewed and observed.

At the same time, as a researcher I was not one of them. Although I participated in many activities, my desire to study multiple sides meant I had to assume a certain detachment or neutrality. Maintaining such detachment was sometimes difficult, particularly where I was present as "experts" misled lay people, and where some groups tried to persuade me to side with them and were disappointed by my distance (see also Douglas 1976; Shupe and Bromley 1980). I had also studied and worked in Sydney in the years 1981 to 1987 and had developed my own professional views, close to that of the group I call consolidationists. However, I persisted in my public neutrality. In part this was a way of protecting my welcome in the various camps, but it was more than a calculated strategy for maintaining access. By putting aside my own position, as much as feasible, I was able to listen to informants' views in a way that would not have been possible if I had taken one side; and having access to opponents' views of each other gave me a much richer sense of the landscape of ideas and actions. As so much professional life is spent where the lines of conflict or confidentiality are already drawn in a way that precludes contact with others, the chance to look at multiple sides was something I did not want to give up. This stance clearly shaped this research.

The most difficult aspects of studying the project, however, were its dispersion through time and space and the resulting infrequency of crucial interactions to observe. The Rouse Hill Development Area is a location created by this planning process, but relatively few people lived there before it was developed and its planning happened in sites scattered across the metropolitan area. People in offices read reports, went to occasional administrative meetings, wrote memos, answered the phone, and tried to keep up with what was happening in other government departments, the Rouse Hill Infrastructure Consortium, and among activists. They planned for a future time and were far less concerned with the site's present condition.

Resident activists ran their daily lives and made a few phone calls, wrote letters, went to meetings, and struggled to keep up with events. All groups read newspapers, watched television, and listened to the radio; but often there were no events to keep up with. Everyone was waiting in their dispersed offices and homes, and going on with other parts of their lives. Face-to-face communication between people with different views was comparatively rare for all those involved but particularly for unpaid activists whose daily lives were filled with other activities. When interactions between different parties did occur they took on special meanings. In these situations people were often interacting for short periods with others who they had already typecast. Although on one level this makes Rouse Hill sound like a leisurely project with plentiful time for planning and public input, this lurching rhythm meant there was – at least in my fieldwork period – enough activity to disrupt other endeavors but often not enough to sustain a high level of interest. For those professionals who had Rouse Hill as part of their job the project was more continuous; however, even for this group it was frequently interspersed with other projects, particularly before construction began. This slow process gave an advantage to those who could write Rouse Hill into their job descriptions.

This kind of dispersed case also raised methodological questions about defining the Rouse Hill project itself. The meaning of the Rouse Hill project was defined and redefined through the planning process. The North West Sector was originally a small bubble on the 1968 plan. The 1984 environmental study however examined a huge area. By the 1989 Regional Environmental Plan the Rouse Hill Development Area took up only a small part of this area deemed suitable for development, an area of 9,400 hectares (Department of Environment and Planning [DEP] 1984a; DoP 1989a; State Planning Authority [SPA] 1968). Public and private responsibilities and interests also shifted through time. In many ways Rouse Hill was more a train of events than a site, although at the same time it was focused on the activity of land development in a particular location. Thus its boundaries were partly geographic, but also boundaries of interest, involvement, and regulation.

As a researcher there to look at the development I found the combination of dispersed geography and the "real time" of urban development at first very frustrating and then, in the end, very interesting. A process that moves forward over such a long period gives great influence to those who can stay with it for the long haul. In chapter four, on the formal planning process, I turn again to this issue.

This research design is closest to the approach called grounded theory. This is a form of exploratory work where a middle range theory is developed from research data, such as the Rouse Hill case study, in contrast to research that uses data to test or illustrate an existing theory (Glaser and Strauss 1967, 32–33). This does not mean that the work is not theoretically informed, but rather that the researcher is open to a variety of theoretical possibilities depending on what emerges from the study.[13] Overall this book analyzes a planning project in multiple ways, exploring its complexity, rather than explaining it through a singular theory.

Study Outline

Looked at from abroad, Australian cities have long been dominated by suburban development, with vast tracts of detached houses. From inside, however, the suburban pattern has periodically been the subject of intense debate. By the early 1990s suburban growth was hotly contested in professional debates, among environmentalists, and in wider government circles. In chapter one I set the context for these debates over growth in Rouse Hill by outlining the history of project and of western Sydney's postwar growth more generally.

In chapter two I examine five major images of good city form articulated in these debates over Rouse Hill. These perspectives were held by professionals and activists as ways of approaching urban development and did not correspond exactly with the positions of agencies and organizations, partly because many agencies experienced internal disagreement. The first group, *expansionists*, had a strong and evocative image of an egalitarian society, inextricably linked to low-density suburbia. Employed by state and local planning agencies, their views had been important in shaping the early conceptualization of Rouse Hill from the 1960s through the early 1980s, and the group was still vocal in the 1990s. For a second group, Rouse Hill was the story of public and private sector *developers* doing their job producing housing they could sell. In Rouse Hill the developers were faced with a difficult situation of increasing infrastructure and financing costs, and a sophisticated range of growth opponents. This was the group where an image of the city was most clearly linked to a set of "interests." A third group, *scientific environmentalists*, had a regional and long-term approach to environmental problems without a strong concern for social issues. Represented among environmental professionals, including some planners inside and outside of government, this group relied on technical information and broadly scientific techniques. In contrast, *local environmentalists* were residents directly affected by the Rouse Hill development. Often recently arrived, they were articulate and motivated to save their "natural" surroundings. The final group, *consolidationists*, were a younger set of planners and human service professionals in state and local government, and some non-profit groups, favoring compact, mixed-use development as a way of solving the environmental, social, and financing problems of suburban development. They were also concerned that the shift away from nuclear families indicated a need for housing forms beyond the detached house.

Explanations of planning conflicts have frequently put these kinds of differences in ideas down to differences in interests, information, or to problems with leadership. Often the explanations divide conflicts into two sides. In Rouse Hill, however, people with the same interests and access to the same information still disagreed. Although perspectives did reflect characteristics such as owning land in the area and professional involvement, the positions were much more than mere translations of these interests. Rather the frameworks linked beliefs about the nature of human life in cities with conceptions of the city forms that could best support those lives and that could be practically achieved. Opposing views were often equally sincere attempts to evaluate competing claims, to reflect on the lessons of past experience, and to make sense of the changing city. While there were a limited number of positions there were certainly more than two sides (see also Schwarz and Thompson 1990).

This second chapter analyzes some of the reasons for disagreement among groups. It draws on Mannheim (1952) to explore generational effects. It then examines how personal experiences, including gendered family experiences, shaped perspectives; describes how the ritualized character of interaction in meetings and the media structured how ideas were represented and worked against consensus; and outlines informants' own views on the reasons for disagreement. From time to time alliances were formed based on shared views of good urban form, that is agreement was forged about outcomes if not underlying principles.

In chapter three I examine one part of this debate in more depth; a set of metaphors used in arguments about Rouse Hill. In the early 1990s, Rouse Hill's and Sydney's futures were frequently imagined in terms of three other cities: as heading toward becoming a Los Angeles, a Toronto, or a Canberra. The chapter outlines how these images were used in the growth debates and how they shaped people's actions by highlighting and obscuring different possibilities. Linked strongly to media images of the places, these city metaphors also left space for action by those planning and protesting the development.

Although Rouse Hill is an actual location, a hill, to the north west of Sydney, the "Rouse Hill Development Area" is a political artifact created through a planning process. The fourth chapter describes how the development area was created out of a set of events partly structured by this formal planning process of metropolitan, regional, and then local plans; of environmental studies, and environmental impact statements. As problems developed and costs rose the formal planning process continued to provide an overall structure and to set the agenda. The problems that emerged over the decades of planning tended to be perceived as severe enough for action only one at a time. This allowed property developers and bureaucrats to incrementally adjust the planning enough for Rouse Hill's first stage to go on, but in a way that eroded its original purposes.

Chapter five examines how the planning process was increasingly privatized, focusing on two coalitions involved in developing Rouse Hill: the Rouse Hill Infrastructure Consortium (RHIC) and the Rouse Hill Community Planning Team (RHCPT). Addressing physical and social infrastructure respectively, they shared similar starting points inspired, at least partly, by public servants interested in continuing infrastructure policies after privatization. The coalitions were both lobby groups and alternative providers of services. Each had, however, unequal access to political and economic resources, and to information and administrative power, inequalities that led to their having quite different impacts on the Rouse Hill development. The Rouse Hill Infrastructure Consortium, able to finance hundreds of millions of dollars worth of infrastructure, pushed the development through numerous obstacles. The Rouse Hill Community Planning Team, in contrast, struggled to provide and lobby for the most basic human services. In Rouse Hill privatization involved a complex set of activities with uneven impacts on social and physical infrastructure even within a single development.

Finally, in chapter six, I return to examine three general issues raised by the Rouse Hill development: the effects that talk and ideas had on urban form; the prominence of claims to rationality, holism, and balance in growth debates; and the conflicts between ideas of what was right to do and the scope of job descriptions.

End Notes

[1] Rationality has been hotly debated in planning circles and has been variously defined as a kind of process (e.g. formal rationality) and a kind of outcome (e.g. social or substantive rationality). In the debates I observed, "rational" seemed to mean something like "better," "correct," or "sensible."

[2] Decentralization, or deconcentration to some North Americans, was eventually revisited with some minor decentralization to Wollongong and Newcastle becoming part of the 1995 metropolitan plan (DoP 1995).

[3] Mandelbaum (1997, 231) – reviewing recent plans from Los Angeles, Toronto, and New York – calls these the "great cosmopolitan themes in contemporary planning debates: the global economy, regionalism, cultural diversity, immigration, institutional competence, privatization, fiscal federalism, and the reconciliation of economic growth, environmental protection, and equity."

[4] By focusing on a large planning project this work joins a number of other studies stretching from Orlan's (1953) account of developing the British new town of Stevenage, and Meyerson and Banfield's (1955) study of public housing location decisions in Chicago, through more recent work by Peattie (1987) on planning the industrial growth pole Ciudad Guayana, and Marris (1987) on community development projects and the London Docklands (see also Clavel 1983; Dalton 1989; McLoughlin 1992).

[5] Some of the critiques and analyses of the idea of the public interest include Altshuler (1965, chapter 5), Howe (1992), Klosterman (1978), Meyerson and Banfield (1955), and Simmie (1974, chapter 5). Friedmann (1987, chapter 1) points to the connection between the public interest and social rationality. I have conceptualized perspectives on urban form as ethical as they provide answers to the Socratic question 'how should one live?' (Williams 1985, 1). The small but growing empirical literature on planning ethics provided a starting point for this research (e.g. Baum 1983; Feld and Hohman 1989; Hendler 1991, 1995; Howe 1994; Howe and Kaufman 1979, 1981; Thomas and Healey 1991). The work has tended to focus on only one or two sides of a conflict, or else more abstractly on generic situations, but was nonetheless useful. Particularly relevant was recent work by Forester (1992, 1993), Hillier (1993), and Throgmorton (1996) analyzing stories told by planners, or in planning

situations, for their ethical content. Also useful was more general social scientific work on the limits of social choice theories (Zey 1992).

[6] Discourse is in its most straightforward definition a kind of talk, and I therefore try to avoid using the word when that is all I mean. More technically, the term discourse means the "ensemble of social practices through which the world is made meaningful to oneself and others" (Johnson *et al.* 1994). Meanwhile, "rhetoric is the study of persuasive discourse" including work on stylistic devices such as metaphor (Johnson *et al.* 1994).

[7] Another body of research was also useful, that looking at more popular perceptions of planning issues. Pincetl's (1992) study of growth control in Pasadena focused on debates over the benefits of growth, exploring alliances between groups that were otherwise at odds (see also Tauxe 1995). A famous series of studies by planners had non-planners map or describe existing cities (Appleyard 1976; Banerjee and Baer 1984; Lynch 1960). Researchers in both North America and Britain had also used more sociological methods to examine conflicts over growth, analyzing the differences between those supporting and opposing growth (e.g. Dubbinck 1984; Evans 1988; Orlans 1953; Spain 1993; cf. Hummon 1986). This group generally found that newer residents were likely to oppose growth.

[8] There is a large literature on language, discourse, and planning including some historical work (Boyer 1983). Generally, however, research has focused on fairly contemporary planning processes (Forester 1989; Grant 1994; Green and Zinke 1993; Howe 1994; Mandelbaum 1990a, 1990b; Marris 1987; McCloskey 1985, 1990; Moore Milroy 1989; Nelson *et al.* 1987; Rydin and Myerson 1989; Tett and Wolfe 1991; Throgmorton 1996; Till 1993).

[9] In this I have also been influenced by Marris (1996, 1) who emphasizes power as the control of uncertainty, creating "a way of thinking about power which emphasizes control over contingencies rather than control over resources." He explores how the power to manage and control uncertainty is unequally distributed in society and, as people compete to protect their freedom of action, the weakest are further burdened. Society as a whole becomes less reciprocal and uncertainty increases.

[10] Pilot interviews and a "suburban soiree" with half a dozen professionals were conducted in June, 1991, in Adelaide.

[11] For comparison, Perin's *Everything in its Place: Social Order and Land Use in America* was based on taped interviews with approximately 20 people, and a taped meeting between six people, as well as a number of documents and her own professional (planning) career (Perin 1977, 17–18). Fainstein (1994, 17) interviewed a total of around 100 people in two cities. Powell (1993, iv) in a study of western Sydney life, relied heavily on newspaper accounts as well as experiences from her own life.

[12] I indented transcriptions or marked them with quotation marks. I have not used page numbers in interview quotes as I used a computer to search for text. My spelling in transcripts is US spelling to conform with the rest of the text. I apologize to any interviewees who may find it odd to see themselves talking in "American." In all but the largest public meetings, where explaining my

purpose would have seemed very odd, I was quite open about my project in researching the debates over Rouse Hill.

[13] This gave me some surprises. Given my interest in ideas about good urban form, I had thought that the categories used by analytical philosophers in examining ethics, and that Howe (1994) had used in empirical work based on interviews, would be easier to distinguish in this kind of case study. I had also been interested in empirical work on ethical reasoning – as opposed to purely theoretical work and surveys. The work of Gilligan and others, for instance, emphasized the diversity of ways in which people made decisions in the moral realm, rather than proposing a universal path (Gilligan 1982; Gilligan *et al.* 1988). Work by Jack and Jack (1989) on the moral orientation of women and men lawyers in the US, and Smith and Valenze (1988) on these orientations in nineteenth century British working-class women, had taken these studies out of experimental situations, grounding them in particular social and historical circumstances. I found however, that in the realm of public policy Gilligan's typology of a morality based on rights and justice, and another on responsibility and care, was hard to find. I was surprised to find that the work of Foucault (1980), on manifold relations of power, and Schwarz and Thompson (1990), on cultural theory, was helpful in analyzing the case.

Chapter One

Big Projects in a Time of Uncertainty: Facing the Future in a Contemporary Urban Development

In 1968 the New South Wales planning agency marked out an oval zone – the North West Sector – on the metropolitan plan for Sydney, Australia. This zone was to be investigated for future development as a growth corridor. By 1994, after the Sector had been recreated as the Rouse Hill Development Area with a planned population of 250,000, the first lots were produced (DoP 1995, 82).

As the growth corridor's planning moved slowly through the decades, the postwar consensus about (sub)urban growth as a social, economic, and environmental benefit was increasingly contested. Some Australians were concerned about regional-scale environmental impacts on water and air quality and called for a moratorium on development and more study. Others wanted to provide suburban homes for a growing trade-up market or for first home buyers, and worked hard to provide innovative financing to allow this. Still others worried about access and isolation and wanted more compact development and better transportation. These debates interrupted the smooth course of suburban development. In 1991, two of the three new inland growth corridors being explored by the New South Wales state government were placed on hold. Only one, Rouse Hill, remained on the government's development program and even it was scaled back almost as soon as the first houses were occupied.[1] In the rest of this chapter I sketch out a history of Rouse Hill's long planning process.

Sydney's Postwar Growth

Sydney, Australia, was founded as a European settlement in 1788. For the next 160 years it grew without the discipline or coordinating vision of a comprehensive plan. After World War Two, like many other cities, Sydney entered the era of formal planning. This account of suburban planning and growth debates is set within a series of metropolitan plans and an elaborate planning bureaucracy. The Australian government structure, with relatively weak local governments, meant that a significant amount of overall planning for Rouse Hill was conducted at the state level.

Sydney is set on a large plain bounded to the east by the ocean and to the north, south, and west by mountains, forests, and waterways (see figure 1). Metropolitan plans for Sydney have been created every twenty years: the 1948 Cumberland Plan (adopted in 1951), the 1968 Sydney Region Outline Plan (SROP), and the 1988 Metropolitan Strategy.[2] In 1995, following early

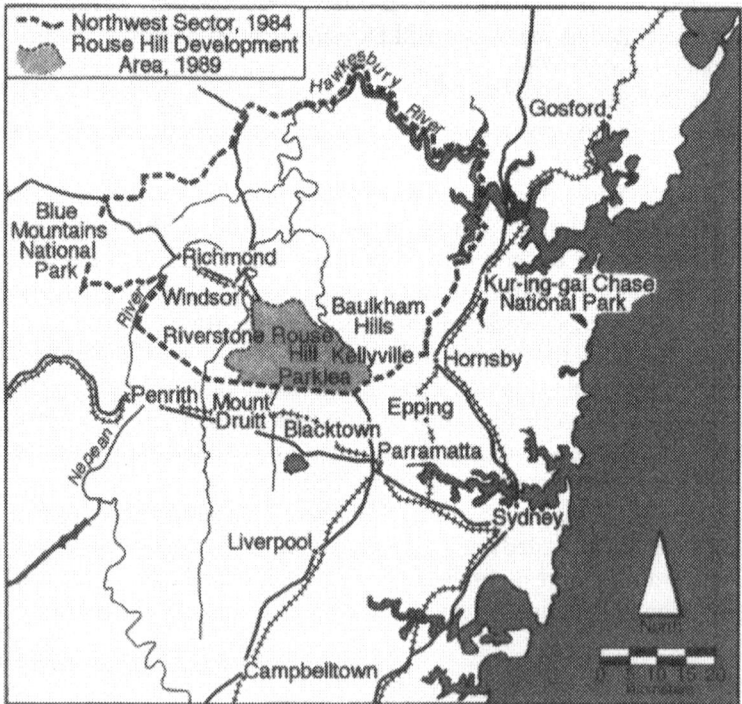

Figure 1 Sydney Region
Map produced by Dave Kvinge.

criticisms of the 1988 plan, a new strategy was published breaking this 20 year cycle. Each plan emulated British and North American planning styles. The 1948 plan proposed freeways, greenbelts, a strong central business district, and a network of district centers. The 1968 plan shifted to a set of principles and policies, giving up the greenbelt and advocating growth along transport corridors along with a network of commercial centers generally located on existing train lines. In 1988 the plan continued the centers emphasis, as well as urban consolidation in the form of some infill and slightly increased fringe densities.[3] The 1995 plan – centered around the goals of equity, efficiency, environmental quality, and livability – called for more stringent consolidation and significantly redirected growth to Newcastle and Wollongong, mid-sized cities to the north and south of Sydney (Winston 1957, 84; SPA 1967, 11). These cities are linked to Sydney by electric trains and freeways, however national parks and difficult topography mean they are quite separate from the Sydney metropolitan area. Each plan encountered difficulties coordinating state and local government agencies, striking the right balance between vision and practicality, and confronting pressure by the development lobby exercised through the state parliamentary cabinet.[4]

Urbanized western Sydney, the location of Rouse Hill, was a product of this postwar era. In 1948 it was largely rural with scattered towns and a population of 210,000 out of a metropolitan figure of 1.6 million (Cumberland County Council 1948, 37). By the early 1990s the west contained large stretches of low density suburbs but most of its area of more than 5,500 square kilometers was not yet urbanized.[5] Its population had expanded to over one million out of a total population of 3.7 million in the Sydney region (DoP 1988, 7; DoP 1995, 126).[6]

Sydney's population growth in the 1980s showed interesting patterns. From mid-1983 to mid-1990 Sydney gained around 248,000 people through immigration from overseas and lost around 140,000 – often Australian-born or long-term residents – through out migration to other parts of Australia (Vipond and Ho 1992, 83). This net gain of 108,000 represented more than two thirds of overall population growth in Sydney with natural increase making up the rest. The outer ring of suburbs experienced 92 percent of this overall population growth, although much of this growth was from Australian residents moving to the western suburbs (Vipond and Ho 1992, 82). There were, however, concentrations of newly arrived overseas immigrants in several parts of western Sydney and these reflected Australia's contemporary immigration stream with many from Asia and the Middle East as well as a decreasing proportion from Europe. As over one fifth of Australia's population were born overseas, nearly three times the US proportion, these immigrant concentrations were not that unusual.[7] However, the 1980s was a period of unusually high immigration, peaking at a net national growth rate of one percent per annum in 1989. It then dropped to under half that figure in the 1990s, a level comparable to the 1970s (McLennan 1996, 77). Given that Sydney was a major settling place for migrants, the high immigration level in the 1980s played a significant part in debates about Rouse Hill.

As in many locations, population and urban growth brought opportunities and problems. This was put quite eloquently by a senior planner opening the Western Sydney Regional Organisation of Councils (WSROC, pronounced "wez-rock") conference on "Western Sydney's Growth – Can We Manage It? ":

> There is a popular image of the growth of Western Sydney as being something unfortunate which has delivered outcomes [to be] accepted or tolerated rather than welcomed. As one who has from childhood lived in Western Sydney, I can see a more mellow version of the "urban sprawl." Without growth and development, centres like Campbelltown, Penrith, Blacktown and above all, Parramatta, would not exist as the lively diverse cities they are today. A great many choices and opportunities we enjoy would not be available... .
> [But t]oday, more vigorously than before, the value and wisdom of Sydney growing by adding more of the same to its edges is being questioned. These questions are being asked by a society very concerned with maintaining and improving its quality of life and its lifestyle; one concerned with the welfare of the environment; and one increasingly prepared to argue in support of its various positions. (McDonald 1991, n.p.)

Project History

Initial planning for Rouse Hill was carried out by the state government planning department (see chronology). Under the 1948 Cumberland Plan the area had been zoned rural as it was largely outside the metropolitan plan's green belt.[8] Rouse Hill, part of a more general area called the North West Sector, was proposed for investigation for urban development in the 1968 metropolitan plan, the Sydney Region Outline Plan. Under the SROP the North West Sector was slated for development only after a number of other areas to the west and south of Sydney (see figure 2).[9] It was given lower priority because of the "high proportion," and thus greater cost, of new physical infrastructure needs (SPA 1968, 21– 22, 83). Rouse Hill, the patch of ground that gives the Rouse Hill Development Area its name, was at that time, and into the period of my fieldwork, a semi-rural area. It is a landscape of market

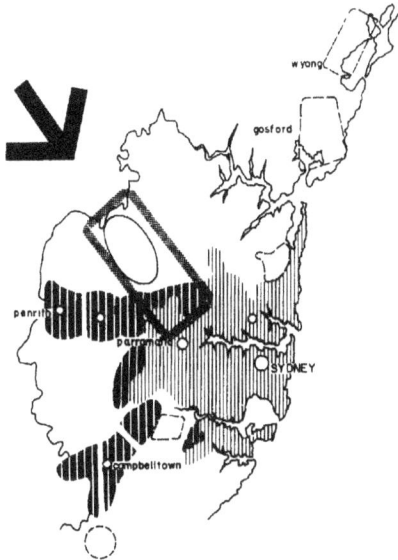

Figure 2 Sydney Region Outline Plan, 1968: Urbanized Area and Sectors with North West Sector Highlighted
Reproduced from the Sydney Region Outline Plan (1968) with permission from the NSW Department of Urban Affairs and Planning, Australia.

gardens and a crematorium, hobby farms and buildings housing small industries; although many of these features will disappear as development progresses. It is the site of a historic building, Rouse Hill House (built 1813–1816), and the probable location of part of the Battle of Vinegar Hill (1804), the earliest convict uprising in Australia. It is also in an area with significant Aboriginal archaeological and rock carving sites (DEP 1984a, section 7; DoP 1989a, 12, 17, 23).

The Sydney Region Outline Plan envisaged the North West Sector providing housing in three areas, although Rouse Hill was the major focus with a proposed population of 370,000 people, a figure reduced in subsequent studies to 250,000 (SPA 1968, 21–22; cf. DoP 1989a).[10] The North West Sector in 1968 spanned three local government areas: Blacktown, the site of large areas of public housing; Baulkham Hills, situated on the western fringe of the more exclusive northern suburbs of Sydney; and Windsor, subsequently renamed Hawkesbury, a more rural area.

While the Sydney Region Outline Plan announced that "change is constant... and the process of changing the plan to meet new conditions must be simple and rapid," it also stated that "in view of the limited extent of the areas for development which are available, there is no alternative to the development of this land when the time is opportune" (SPA 1968, 7, 81). As "guidance to private developers, local councils, and Government Departments and State Instrumentalities" this was a clear indication that change would occur and profits were to be made (SPA 1968, 104).

Internal state government studies of the sector commenced in the early 1980s with the public planning process starting in 1984. In 1981, at the request of the state cabinet, a document called the "North West Sector Structure Plan" was prepared as an internal state government document by the Department of Environment and Planning. (The state planning agency, like many other government agencies, frequently changed its name. For a detailed listing, see abbreviations.) It was presented to the Housing Committee of the state cabinet in early 1982. The "Structure Plan" was a very broad exercise done in the context of a proposal to place a second Sydney metropolitan airport in the area. This was not an officially recognized plan but rather a planning study done for internal purposes.[11] Transportation studies for this plan indicated that full development of the sector (put, by 1982, at 340,000 people) would be extremely expensive and so a truncated sector of 252,000 people was devised in order to reduce costs. This development was to be at a density of 10 lots or 35 persons per gross hectare (DEP 1982, 1, 22–23).

By 1982 a number of public authorities and private developers had already bought land in the area. These included: the state housing authority called the Housing Commission with approximately 600 hectares; and the land banking and development authority, the Land Commission, with 134 hectares. The Housing Commission and Land Commission were amalgamated in 1986 to form the Department of Housing (DoH).[12] By the mid-1980s the state planning agency held 167 hectares around the proposed regional center and there was also a 385 hectare site held for a long period by North Sydney Brick and Tile (DEP 1982, 14, map 5; DEP 1984b, 10). A number of other property developers bought parcels, eventually forming the core of the consortium group I describe in chapter five. This turned out to be one of the last large areas of land banking on the fringe of Sydney (Bird 1991a, 23; Cardew 1985; Daily 1982, chapter 4).

In 1983 a "Medium Term Options Study," prepared by the interdepartmental Urban Development Committee, was in turn presented to the Housing Committee of Cabinet.[13] It recommended development around Rouse Hill in the North West Sector ahead of other major options in western Sydney.[14] The report pointed to four main attractions of the area: lower servicing costs than other remaining areas; attractive natural features; a better chance of attracting employment even given that a large number of residents would be employed outside the sector; and more possibilities for upgrading transport, particularly rail (DEP 1984a, 10–11, 157).

Detailed planning, open to public and local government comment, then commenced and followed a predictable, if slow, sequence under the 1979 Environmental Planning and Assessment Act. The state planning agency prepared a Regional Environmental Study in 1984, followed in 1986 by a Draft Regional Environmental Plan, and in 1989 Regional Environmental Plan. These defind *environmental* planning quite broadly, as general land use planning. The two local councils in the first stage of the Rouse Hill Development Area then took over the planning process preparing local planning instruments for the Parklea and Kellyville-Rouse Hill Release Areas in Blacktown and Baulkham Hills respectively. Draft Local Environmental Plans in 1990 were followed by Local Environmental Plans in 1991, which were broad rezoning instruments. Finally, Development Control Plans prepared in the mid-1990s indicated street layouts.[15] Each study or draft plan was exhibited with submissions sought from the public and other government authorities.[16]

Although coordinated by the state planning agency, the state housing authority and the Water Board were also key players in this planning process as they were involved in physically developing the site. Each had large staffs of hundreds of professionals; the Department of Housing owned and managed 130,000 rental properties in addition to its sale program (DoH 1997). Rouse Hill, of course, was only one of many projects for these departments. Interviews with participants and minutes of meeting indicate work on Rouse Hill was generally conducted by small teams of one to six people, at least some of whom also dealt with other projects.

The two local governments, which were important actors in the later stages, each created a small team of planners and other professionals to work on the project. Blacktown, an area with significant large suburban public housing areas, many with thousands of residents, focused on getting adequate human services and recreational facilities from governments and property developers, and on having them in the early stages of the development (e.g. Pund and Fleming 1997). Baulkham Hills had to deal with an articulate set of residents who were inclined to protest every move, but council staff were also interested in improving subdivision design (Baulkham Hills Council Environmental Services 1993, 1994a, 1994b) (see figures 3 and 4).

This process of formal planning coincided with, and contributed to, a number of controversies over the costs of continued suburbanization and the future shape of Sydney. Key issues included infrastructure pricing, finance, and subsidies, along with water and air pollution. Urban consolidation was proposed as the main alternative to low-density suburban developments like Rouse Hill. This approach argued for planning much new development in existing areas, redeveloped at higher densities, although some more compact expansion would occur on the edge. This policy seemed to some to minimize a number of the economic and environmental costs of growth, although as is explained later this was a matter of heated debate. Given the long history of government support of suburban expansion these debates represented a major rethinking of public policy.

In the postwar period, state governments in Australia have directly provided most infrastructure in new urban areas and have done this on the assumption that first-home owners at the lower end of the market would be the buyers. Infrastructure provision has thus been a form of housing assistance for lower- and middle-income earners buying suburban houses. There has also been significant public housing in the outer suburbs including detached houses, townhouses, and some small-scale, low-rise apartments. This contrasts with the United States where the federal tax deduction for mortgage interest has been a major form of housing subsidy

Figure 3   New Housing, Baulkham Hills
Photograph by the author, 1995.

Figure 4   New Housing, Blacktown
Photograph by the author, 1995.

and where attached units dominate public housing provision. In the early 1990s in Sydney the state Department of Housing expected to develop around 30 percent of land in the fringe Urban Development Program (UDP) release areas. Although UDP areas provide only 40 percent of new housing in Sydney, the Department of Housing was still a significant developer (Department of Health, Housing and Community Services [DHHCS] 1992b, 44, 52).

In the late 1980s, increases in real interest rates made government borrowing to finance infrastructure more expensive. At the same time the federal government lowered the limit on state government borrowing, making it harder to fund large government infrastructure projects. The demographics of home buyers in outer areas also shifted to include more of the move-up market making government, that is taxpayer, infrastructure provision seem like an unnecessary subsidy to the already established.

Meanwhile the only areas left to develop in Sydney, including Rouse Hill, were physically difficult to service and therefore more expensive than previous locations. The Rouse Hill Development Area was placed in a relatively isolated location already subject to high levels of air pollution (Hyde and Johnson 1990). Although a rail line ran through the area it was surrounded by flood plains. Roads needed major augmentation to serve a larger population of commuters. The area was just beyond the ocean outfall system for sewage treatment that much of Sydney used and so its effluent and runoff had to drain into the much more fragile Hawkesbury-Nepean River system (Wilson 1990; Water Board 1991b, 7). New environmental requirements, combined with some deterioration in environmental conditions, also increased the overall cost of the development, undermining affordability. With less money to fund infrastructure, and its increasing price tag, Rouse Hill's planning came close to a halt in 1987.

In 1988 a Liberal government replaced Labor at the state level. In this context, the state Department of Housing, owner of 800 hectares in the first stage of Rouse Hill, formed the Rouse Hill Infrastructure Consortium with private developers who were also landowners in the area. They proposed to finance water services privately as these were the major services legally required before land could be released (rezoned) for urban development. This was a controversial proposal.

Privatization allowed the project to proceed, and promised to save the government some expense for water infrastructure and costs to the Department of Housing. Other departments, however, were then required to provide additional services to the area without the same possibility of private sector funding. In an area with very little existing infrastructure, and in a period of high real interest rates, these other infrastructure costs represented a huge expense.

As local government zoning and subdivision planning commenced in the early 1990s, federal interest in urban issues also increased, driven by similar situations across the country. In Sydney, Rouse Hill's environmental and financing problems became especially critical, feeding into wider concerns about the costs of growth. While the Rouse Hill Development Area was only one of many growth areas in Australia, in Sydney it formed an important focus for debates, particularly after the other two large western Sydney growth areas – areas that were not as far along in the planning process – were drastically reduced in size or placed on indefinite hold because of similar economic and environmental problems (DoP 1991a, 1991b, 1991c). An early review of the 1988 metropolitan plan commenced, spurred by these debates over growth (DoP 1993; DoP 1995).

Following the publication of the revised 1995 metropolitan plan it now seems likely that the later stages of Rouse Hill will be delayed for a very long time and possibly canceled altogether (DoP 1995) (see figure 5). Although land for around 23,000 dwellings or 70,000 to 75,000 people was rezoned in Rouse Hill mainly in 1991, in this newest metropolitan plan the rest of the area is again, as in 1968, represented by an oval and labeled as under investigation for development. This new plan deals with a "Greater Metropolitan Region" including Sydney and the coastal cities of Wollongong and Newcastle, and includes significant consolidation of urban areas (DoP 1995,4). Although Sydney already has a large stock of attached dwel-lings, around a third of its housing, this means a further shift away from the cultural ideal of quarter- and eighth-of-an-acre blocks, to houses on smaller lots, townhouses, and apartments (Thorne 1991). This shift in focus from the 1988 plan that essentially filled in the previously undeveloped areas, clearly reflects the debates analyzed in this volume. While other cities in Australia have not yet reached the kind of physical limits and high infrastructure prices Sydney has been encountering, Rouse Hill's problems do seem indicative of the future shape of urban development, part of a new round of developments involving far more difficult and contested tradeoffs (National Housing Strategy [NHS] 1991d, 66).

These controversies over infrastructure, water quality, and air pollution were still unfolding in 1991 and 1992 when I undertook the fieldwork for this study. There were many public meetings to attend and even a housing design competition with Rouse Hill as a competition site (Next Move 1991). A series of initiatives by all levels of government, sometimes in conjunction with industry groups, was also focusing on the future of urban development in Australian cities. The federal government conducted inquiries, strategies, and conferences on housing, social justice, ecologically sustainable development,[17] and patterns of urban

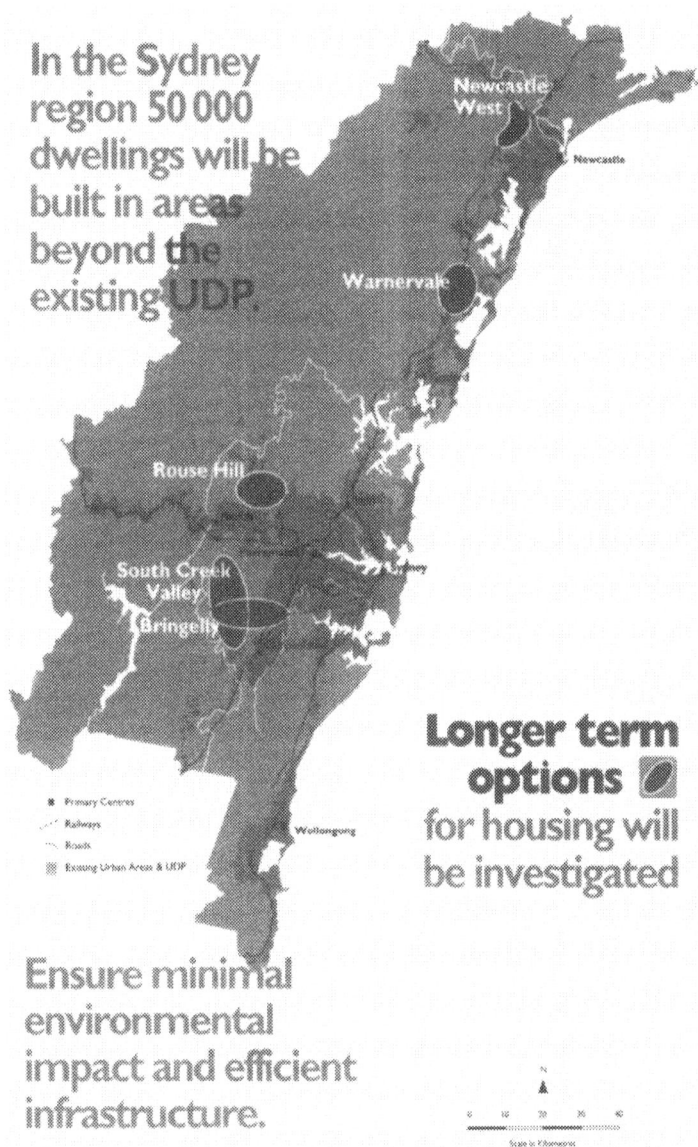

In the Sydney region 50 000 dwellings will be built in areas beyond the existing UDP.

Newcastle West

Newcastle

Warnervale

Rouse Hill

South Creek Valley

Bringelly

Sydney

Longer term options 🖾
for housing will be investigated

Primary Centres
Railways
Roads
Existing Urban Areas & UDP

Wollongong

Ensure minimal environmental impact and efficient infrastructure.

N

Scale in Kilometres

Figure 5 Longer-Term Housing Options, 1995 Metropolitan Plan
Reproduced from Cities for the 21st Century (1995) with permission from the
NSW Department of Urban Affairs and Planning, Australia.

settlement.[18] A background report for the National Housing Strategy explicitly considered urban form and development strategies (Minnery 1992).[19] One of the four federal Building Better Cities projects in New South Wales, announced in 1992, incorporated bus priority lanes to Rouse Hill as part of a model project (DHHCS 1992c, 12-13).[20]

Reports from the various inquires and programs were used by people involved in Rouse Hill in their deliberations and arguments. Rouse Hill's history was thus both a fairly ordinary, if slow-moving, example of large-scale development, but also coincided with a period where some aspects of urban development were being dramatically reconsidered in a public debate.

This discussion, finally, requires a note about the words "urban," "suburban," and "city," that I have been using as partial synonyms in a way that is unusual in the United States. Australians, particularly Australians involved in housing and urban development, used the terms suburbs and suburban in a particular way. "Suburbs" were small geographical units with a name and could found across the metropolitan area, somewhat comparable to the US term "neighborhood." Often they had a separate postal code but they were generally not equivalent to a local government area; local government areas were made up of many suburbs, and the Sydney metropolitan area was made up of nearly 50 local government areas. Suburbs were highly differentiated and generally were specified as inner suburbs (or the inner city), middle-ring suburbs, and outer or fringe suburbs, moving outward from the historical core of the metropolitan area. "*The* suburbs" was used as a term by planners to mean areas of detached housing generally not right in the middle of the city. The development of outer suburbs was more likely to be called "urban development" than "suburban development." In Australia, outer suburbs are very mixed in income with many outer suburban areas developed for first-home buyers and many containing significant amounts of public housing. Thus the Rouse Hill project was an urban development, in the outer ring of suburbs.

End Notes

1   In the 1995 metropolitan plan one of the other sectors, South Creek Valley, was again marked for investigation, along with future stages of Rouse Hill.

2   The first metropolitan plan was prepared by the Cumberland County Council. Its successor agency, the State Planning Authority prepared the 1968 plan; and one of its successors, the Department of Environmental and Planning, reviewed it (see DEP 1980). By the time of the 1988 plan the agency's name was the Department of Planning.

3   Densities were increased from 8 lots per gross hectare to 10 (DoP 1988).

4   Each metropolitan plan had a mix of successes and failures: the Cumberland Plan grossly underestimated population growth, the Sydney Region Outline Plan overestimated, and so the 1988 Metropolitan Strategy avoided the issue by planning for a future population of 4.5 million but not stating the date when it would reach that population. A number of historians have assessed these successes and failures (see Freestone 1992; Parker and Troy 1972; Sandercock 1990; Spearitt and DeMarco 1988; Winston 1957).

5   Western Sydney is defined here as the Western Sydney Regional Organisation of Councils (WSROC) area. Perhaps because WSROC produced and popularized a variety of data on the area of western Sydney within its boundaries, this was perhaps the most common professional definition. This definition, however, excluded the south western councils of Camden, Campbelltown, and Wollondilly. Moreover, in census terms the Western Sydney Statistical Subdivision included the Local Government Area of Auburn (which left WSROC in 1980). From 1979 WSROC, however, also contained Liverpool (see DEP 1984a, 121; WSROC no date).

6   The figure of 1.6 million in 1947 represented the population of the contiguous urban area, however the regional population, defined by the County of Cumberland, numbered 1.7 million the rest of whom lived on farms and in towns and villages (Cumberland County Council 1948, 37). By 1991 urbanization had largely swallowed up the separate farms, towns, and villages and so the difference between the County and urban population was not as significant.

7   Various researchers and planning documents referred to this massive growth both in Australia as whole and in western Sydney in particular (Collins 1988; DEP 1984a, 121; Fulop and Sheppard 1988, 610; Fagan 1986, 12).

8   This plan was technically prepared by the Cumberland County Council and not a state authority, but this was a precursor to the state planning agencies.

9   The areas were, going from west to south: the West Sector, Hoxton Park-Fairfield, South West Sector, and Menai (SPA 1968).

10 In this plan Rouse Hill was called Rouse Hill-Maralya (SPA 1968, 21–22).

11 The officially recognized plans defined under the 1979 Environmental Planning and Assessment (EP&A) Act include: State Environmental Planning Policies (SEPPs), Regional Environmental Plans (REPs), Local Environmental Plans (LEPs), and Development Control Plans (DCPs) (NSW 1979).

12 The Housing Commission had operated throughout the postwar period and provided public housing, mostly for rent. The Land Commission was set up in

1975 at the instigation of the Whitlam Labor government as a public land bank to decrease market speculation and fluctuations in land supply.

[13] The Urban Development Committee, set up in 1980, had representatives from twenty state agencies with the state planning authority as chair. It prepared the Urban Development Program, a rolling five year program of land releases (DHHCS 1992b, 41). It coordinated social and physical infrastructure provision with planning and land acquisition, and generally advised the Minister for Planning on growth issues (DEP 1948b,4). The Urban Development Committee had number of subcommittees including Human Services, Transport, Local Government, Physical Services and Land Assembly, and Urban Consolidation (Lang 1990, 94). For part of the 1980s it also had a North West Sector Sub-committee.

[14] The other options at this time were: Riverstone-Schofields area in the northern part of the North West Sector; Austral in Bringelly, later called South Creek Valley; and two versions of Macarthur South (to the south of the South West Sector) (DEP 1983, 2–3).

[15] The Regional Environmental Study, Draft Regional Environmental Plan, and Regional Environmental Plan were prepared by the state planning agency in "close consultation with" the North West Sector Sub-Committee (in 1984 and 1986) and Rouse Hill Development Area Sub-Committee (in 1989) of the Western Sydney Planning and Development Committee. These Sub-Committees included representatives from Local Government Areas (Penrith, Hornsby, Hawkesbury, Blacktown, and Baulkham Hills in 1984 and 1986, the latter three in 1989), the Western Sydney Regional Organization of Councils (WSROC) (1986, 1989), and various state government departments (DEP 1984a, 261; 1986a, n.p.; DoP 1989a, n.p).

[16] This process created quite a pile of reports (see DEP 1984a, 1986a; DoP 1989a; Baulkham Hills Shire Council 1990, 1991; Blacktown City Council 1990, 1991).

[17] The term "sustainable development" comes from the 1987 Bruntland Report *Our Common Future* (Bruntland Commission 1987). This report emphasized both ecological and economic goals. In Australia the sustainability debate was generally specified as ecological sustainability. Economic issues were either subsumed into this debate or seen as widely separate.

[18] Federal conferences, reports, and lectures were quite diverse (see Commonwealth Environmental Protection Agency 1992; DHHCS 1992a; Edwards 1991; Howe 1991; NHS 1991a, 1991b, 1991c, 1991d, 1992; Throsby 1991). Paul Keating, just before becoming Prime Minister, also entered the debate (Keating 1991).

[19] Minnery (1992) analyzed seven "archetypal" urban forms: current low density, more compact cities, nodes or centers within the existing urban fabric (also know as urban villages or district centers), linear or corridor growth, regional cities, twin cities or growth poles, and an (even more) spread out city. This was not the only Australian work examining alternative city forms. In New South Wales the Australian Institute of Urban Studies produced a report on transport and urban form analyzing three scenarios: likely (urban sprawl), possible (high-density urban villages), and desirable (a combination) (Simons and Black 1992).

This echoed work in the mid-1970s by the then federal Cities Commission (1975) as well as by the West Australian and Victorian governments in the early 1990s (cited in Minnery 1992, 16–17).

[20] The Building Better Cities Program was announced in 1991 by the federal Labor government with $816 million budgeted for model projects over five years.

CHAPTER TWO

Five Images of a Suburb: Competing Perspectives on the Economy, Environment, and Family Life

This chapter explores some of the ways that groups of generally middle-class people – planning, development, and human service professionals; environmental activists; and local residents – talked about Rouse Hill. Five major visions of good city form ran through the messages I collected from these groups during my fieldwork. I call these perspectives expansionists, developers, scientific environmentalists, local environmentalists, and consolidationists (see figure 6).

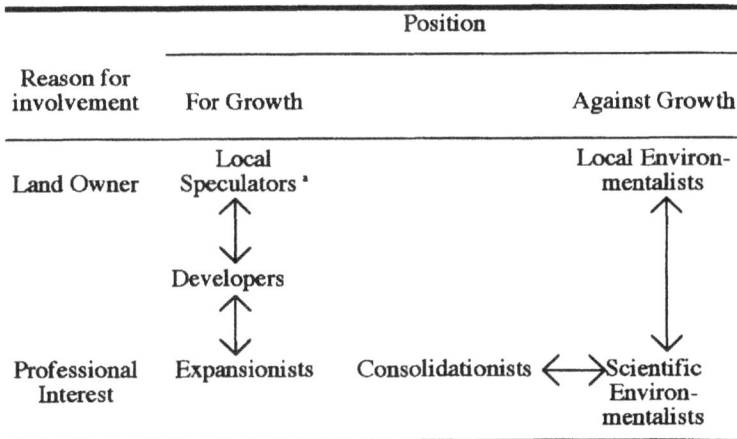

	Position		
Reason for involvement	For Growth		Against Growth
Land Owner	Local Speculators [a] ↑↓ Developers ↑↓		Local Environmentalists ↑
Professional Interest	Expansionists	Consolidationists ⟷	Scientific Environmentalists

a. This is a sixth group not dealt with in detail.
⟷ Two party alliances.

Figure 6   Perspectives and Frameworks

39

In the context of often heated debates over growth, some ideas crystallized into frameworks or perspectives. An image of popular, inevitable, egalitarian suburban growth set the framework for the project in the 1960s. This framework remained important into the 1990s, being drawn on by public and private sector developers and some planners. In the 1990s, however, environmental concerns about sustainability and economic concerns about affordability provided alternative perspectives that started to slow and reshape the development. Low-density suburbs that had seemed natural and egalitarian began to seem environmentally and economically wasteful, at least to some.

I called the ways that people talked about good city form ideas, frameworks, or perspectives, because other words seemed either too vague (attitudes, norms, preferences), too loaded with judgements about their truth (ideologies), or too formal and coherent (ethics, morals). I also wanted to keep the term *stories* as a more general word for the various kinds of stories it was possible to tell about Rouse Hill as exemplified by this book's central chapters. I use the word *image* to mean both these frameworks and perspectives and the more metaphorical portrayals of the development; for example, as being like Los Angeles.

Groups drew on a variety of sources in constituting their frameworks including interests, their past experiences, and beliefs about the future. The frameworks were not necessarily coherent and consistent at all levels. They were often more of a collage of ideas made and remade from the residues of past experiences, traditions, and insights, that were formulated and reformulated in the public debates about growth.

Previous studies approached this issue of classifying perspectives in a number of ways. Some used self identification in highly polarized situations such as the abortion debate (Ginsburg 1989; Krasniewicz 1992). Others used professional training or job descriptions.[1] Orlans (1953, 132ff.), in an early study of the Stevenage new town in England, categorized people by their "rational interests" and "motives or arguments" leading to a long and uneven list of such groups as the: agricultural interest, rural cult, property interest, planning versus freedom, Residents Protection Association, and so on. My categorization is closer to that of Pynoos (1986) who created categories related to bureaucratic style: traditionalists, reformers, survivalists, and avoiders. It also echoes Hummon (1986) who developed a quite complex typology of popular perspectives on urban life: villagers, suburban villagers, suburban enthusiasts, urban suburbanites, temporary and transitional urbanites, local urbanists, and cosmopolitan urbanists.

The categories I created for the frameworks also follow those that some of my informants made in the process of working on or protesting the project.[2] Only one group name, developers, exactly corresponds to that used in the actual case; this was the only group where a perspective cleanly matched an interest. However, to avoid confusion I use the terms *property* developer or *public* and *private sector* developer, to indicate the social role rather than the perspective. In the cases of other frameworks I use names that are sympathetic with the various groups' self-understandings and self-representations. For example, one informant divided environment activists into two groups – "real" and "fake" – a division that I have represented with the terms *scientific environmentalist* and *local environmentalist*. Interestingly, all five groups contained people trained as urban and regional planners, although they were more concentrated among expansionists, consolidationists, and scientific environmentalists. The state planning agencies contained both expansionists and consolidationists in their Rouse Hill teams, environmental agencies included consolidationists and scientific environmentalists, infrastructure agencies an even wider variety including developers and scientific environmentalists. It is important to emphasize that these groups shared common perspectives rather than interests, professional training, institutional affiliation, or social role. Two other groups had a less vocal or organized role in the debate and are not included in the analysis. Local speculators were local landowners who accepted development and focused their efforts on channeling it in locally advantageous ways. Various intellectuals often prided themselves on having idiosyncratic views.

The frameworks I located were not static. At different times stories or frameworks gained and lost popularity and people sometimes moved between them. The frameworks themselves developed through time as situations and perceptions changed. While the frameworks evolved and often lacked detail, they staked out the contested ground in a way that was relatively stable. In addition, few attempts were made to promote compromise, rather groups took a more adversarial approach toward alternative views.

This chapter takes the frameworks at one point in their history, the early 1990s, examining their content and structure, and outlining their approach to urban form and the politics of urban development. In outlining each perspective I start with quotes that provide a broad overview of the position. I then analyze the structure of its argument, its knowledge base, its concept of community and society, and its ultimate vision of a good city. Positions varied in their level of coherence about each of these areas and the descriptions that follow reflect this unevenness. As some people were more articulate and succinct than others the quotes that follow reflect this subset of interviewees. The descriptions also weave together interviews with published accounts, although these sources are always clearly distinguished. The chapter concludes by analyzing differences among perspectives. Differences were articulated in several areas: in terms of the importance and character of environmental and economic issues; through differing interpretations of which urban forms were practically achievable; through debates over forms of knowledge, particularly pitting local against professional views; and by variations in the geographic and social scope of professional, or activist, concern and responsibility. Underlying these more readily articulated issues were a range of assumptions about the character of individual lives and of their realtions in society. In explaining their own underlying assumptions, professionals and social activists talked surprisingly often about their family history, a history patterned by generation and gender rather than simple interests. However, when describing why others disagreed with them their explanations were far more diverse.

Expansionists

One way to read Rouse Hill was an expansionist's dream environment:

> Low-density suburbia is really synonymous with a very
> egalitarian community and in fact if there's one thing
> Australia has achieved in its two hundred years is [that]
> it's the most egalitarian society, which is absolutely

fantastic. And some of the baggage that goes with that is low-density housing, because Australia has, as you know, the highest home ownership, higher than America. And that is recognized throughout the world as a great tick [i.e. check]. That's a great social tick, and it has achieved that. And low-density or detached housing is again synonymous with house ownership.

It's very hard to, it's not as pleasant to own a home unit under strata [i.e. condominium] title and all that with [homeowner associations] as it is your own house. So that's been easy, that's been the desire, that's been why people desire that. And that's been good, and in fact it has allowed a working class for the first time ever in the English-speaking world to own something. When they die they have 200,000 dollars they can pass on to their children which has allowed the next generation to buy something as well. I mean it's an incredible success story. And this is a physical manifestation of that. And so suburbia from that point of view is great. (Frank, interview)

Expansionists had a strong and evocative image of an egalitarian society, inextricably linked to low-density suburbia.[3] Their views had been important in shaping the early conceptualization of Rouse Hill from the 1960s through the early 1980s. Their broad argument was that suburban growth promoted equality as it provided access for the working class to the highest quality form of housing. This perspective echoed the work of contemporary Australian academics such as Hugh Stretton and Patrick Troy (e.g. Troy 1996). In this passage from *Housing and Government,* the 1974 Boyer Lectures broadcast nationally on radio by the then Australian Broadcasting Commission, Stretton outlined the expansionists' basic tenets.

The figures show at least three kinds of winners in the international housing stakes. First there are the countries that build the most housing – the biggest houses with the most rooms, the most space per head of population, the most houses with private gardens. Overlapping with that group there are the countries with the highest proportion of home owners (whether they own houses or flats or caravans). Third are the countries

*which distribute their housing best; give their people
the most equal shares of private indoor and outdoor
space.*

*Very few countries are near the top on all three
counts, and the best of the few are Australia, New
Zealand and Norway. (Stretton 1974, 9)[4]*

Although expansionists admitted that greenfield suburban development led to some problems, particularly access to jobs and
services in the early years, these drawbacks were essentially short-
term, a minor tradeoff in providing the best form of housing on a
large scale. Although temporary, this situation of poor initial planning and servicing was still a concern. It led expansionists to re-
state the 1948 Cumberland Plan stressing housing and social
service standards that were vital for a "full" family life: roads,
drainage, libraries, public pools, restaurants, medical care, access
to cultural events in the center city, and access for "the male of the
house ... to go out and earn a few bucks to buy luxuries like bread
and milk and theater tickets" (Thomas, interview; see also Cumberland Country Council 1948, 67).

Expansionists also pointed out that by the 1990s the deficits of
services and facilities that had plagued the growth of Sydney were
in the process of being eradicated in many fringe suburban areas.
People could now make their entire lives on the edge.

*That's what suburbia ought to be is its own little city,
and it's happening if everybody lets it happen. And it's
happening, but half the people who criticize it have
never been there, wouldn't even know where it was... .
I've worked too much in the area, I've worked in the
[outer suburbs, the] Mount Druitts and Campbelltowns.
There's a place for everybody. I mean people there like
it. (Frank, interview)*

*And lots of people are very happy living out this way.
The people out at [exurban] Wollondilly way... they'd
think you were mad if you said you were going into
[central] Sydney today, down to all that smog. And out
here you've got beautiful bushlands and water... . (Thomas, interview)*

As competent practitioners with a broad knowledge of practice both within Australia and overseas, expansionist planners supported Rouse Hill as the best remaining option for Sydney's growth and an exciting chance to build a new city. They talked about "doing a Canberra," replicating Australia's national capital, to provide "homes for the people." Like most of those involved in Rouse Hill, they were concerned about its cost but hoped that this would not prove an insurmountable problem, even if that involved extensive government funding.

> *If something goes awry and the state government's got to come good with 100 million or so [to bail out the consortium], which is really not very much for a state government, [I hope] that they'd be prepared to do that to keep the show on the road. Because if they fail it's not just a matter of them being portrayed as bad managers, it means there's not homes for the people, and that's the bottom line, that's what it's all about, the whole exercise. Everything is combined to get some bloke [i.e. man] with a roof over his head so his family can grow up in reasonable surroundings. And that's what it's all about, and that's the only thing ... . (Thomas, interview)*

Clearly expansionists believed that the government should support homes for "people" of a particular sort – nuclear families – and in a particular form of "reasonable surroundings" – low-density suburban dwellings. In this perspective, cities, or at least their outer suburbs, were fundamentally places of access; access for male breadwinners in nuclear families to jobs, and access for the rest of the family to a variety of services and cultural activities.

In the 1991 Australian census married couple families with children under 18 made up just over one third of Australian households, and in 1990 the US figure was just over one quarter,[5] so these kinds of families are almost as rare in Australia as in the US. Expansionists occasionally mentioned that other household types existed; however, the nuclear family form was dominant for this group. Expansionists certainly revealed a rich and complex understanding of the details of these families' daily lives, an understanding that they explained was based on both their professional experience and their experiences as members of nuclear families. Absent from their description was any discussion of other kinds of relationships

and access; to wider social networks of friends and extended family,
or of organizational memberships.

The expansionists ended the 1980s thinking that they worked
within a broad Australian consensus about suburban housing. However, their vision was increasingly challenged by those worried
about the social and environmental costs of growth. With their
appeal to popular support no longer so certain or obvious, they
responded by pointing to the inevitability of growth. As one senior
planner explained in answer to my question about why people disagreed with their position on growth:

> *They're looking at things very simplistically, and of course
> they have no answers, they have no answers. The only
> answer they've got is "stop Sydney growing" or "let them
> go to the established areas" or, you know, "try harder
> on urban consolidation." All those things which if you
> really know about urban issues you'll realize there's no
> quick fix ... . So you almost have to give a complete town
> planning course to these people who are the critics be-
> cause they can't see the total picture and that's the prob-
> lem and that's up to government to articulate that, to get
> it over to people. (Frank, interview)*

Expansionists were either suspicious of or doubtful about attempts
to avoid the economic or environmental costs of suburban sprawl by
increasing densities. In their eyes, the higher-density solution was a
lower-quality solution. They agreed that expansion was costly.
Expansionists argued, however, that the alternative strategy of consolidation would involve even more expensive replacement and upgrading of infrastructure in existing areas. Although resigned to some
increases in developer charges for infrastructure, they were concerned
that these were already increasing too much and too fast, excluding
lower-income groups from owning detached houses. Similarly, they
argued that threats to the environment need not stop growth. Some
problems such as water pollution were amenable to technical solutions – "it just costs money" (Frank, interview). Other more intractable problems such as air pollution linked to automobile dependence
were not really the severe problems portrayed by environmentalists,
rather they were acceptable costs of mobility.

Thus this group were populist and pragmatic: people wanted
suburbs and should have them. They also had a basic commitment

to an ideal of fairness, realized as government-supported access to suburban homes for all income groups. The expansionists' desired outcome reflected a long tradition of urban development in Australia. They appealed to a set of common understandings about growth and development, but these common understandings came under increasing criticism as Rouse Hill's development progressed.

Developers

A second reading of Rouse Hill was as a story of developers doing their job producing serviced land and housing: "Obviously the Department of Housing's interest is to develop land; it has this charter in life to do that. The private developers that were involved... had the same sort of goal" (Gregory, interview).

Although the private sector developers were concerned about housing sales, and the public sector had both sale and rental programs, the cultures of the public and private sector professionals were quite similar. For both groups the crucial issues were:

> *The timing of the development of the land, [and] keeping costs of development down. And I guess timing is driven by the money where if there's no money you can't do it anyway... . The cost is driven by what's necessary to service the area for release, but also, it's also influenced by what's the minimum acceptable service requirement. (Timothy, interview)*

In Rouse Hill the developers were faced with increasing production and financing costs, and a sophisticated range of growth opponents. They had changed their practices significantly in the late 1980s in response to this changing development context, although this occurred in only a limited number of areas essential for government approval of the land rezoning and development. They focused on providing mandated physical infrastructure and on lowering costs. They spent a great deal of effort in figuring out the water and road infrastructure financing and trying to minimize the cost of environmental regulations. They were also primarily focused on housing development and were not much interested in creating "lifestyle" developments that included significant additional services and facilities.

When asked about the future of Sydney's urban development they talked about more of the same, fringe growth, although infill development would become increasingly accepted as "the current fears about overcrowding and poorly designed products" were overcome (Timothy, interview). As one professional continued:

> *I'm trying to think what my view is on urban development and I think that, in a nutshell, it's that urban development on the fringe is certainly going to be the major area of satisfying the demand for increasing growth. I don't think there's any question of that. Urban consolidation will have a role in it but not anywhere near as major as people seem to make out. That's purely because people don't want to live that sort of lifestyle; some people do, a lot of people don't. (Timothy, interview)*

Like expansionists, developers were critical of the recent ascendance of environmental issues in public debates, an ascendance that had led to policies that they believed would be unbalanced in the long-term. While acknowledging that the environmental issues in western Sydney would seriously constrain future growth, and had already changed its form, the developers' stance emphasized technical solutions to environmental problems. Further, in the short-term, the goal of providing housing overrode the more difficult environmental issues such as air pollution.

> *I think that on the environmental side a lot of the desires that people have are quite commendable, and I think they're certainly supported by not all developers but certainly most developers, and by most sensible people. But there's practical reality as well. Now ... a number of environmental groups are now pushing for no development in western Sydney, and that's a very commendable goal. But the only problem there is [that] people are still moving into Sydney, and Sydney's still growing, and until you can work out a way to stop that you've got to put them somewhere. So there's a practical reality somewhere short of the ideal, and I guess that's one of the most difficult things to balance ... . The environmental issues have really, really arisen over the last*

couple of years, in fact probably only in the past 18
months, and they really have become fairly big issues.
And well that's evident from the fact that all the other
urban release areas in Sydney have now been stopped,
and I think that's a mistake. (Timothy, interview)

While not particularly happy with privately financed infrastructure – it would have been far cheaper and easier for them if the government footed the whole bill – the developers saw it as the only way to develop land quickly in troubled times. However, unlike the expansionists who were committed to low-density fringe growth, developers were also open to the emerging government requirement for more compact development as long as it would sell. As one developer explained in reply to my questions about how his ideas were formed about good suburban development:

I think my ideas are changing all the time ... . I think
[they have] been changing in terms of the role that the
environmental sort of areas need to play in it, I mean ...
planning a development so you minimize the environ-
mental impact. That's always been a goal, I suppose,
but I take it a lot more, I don't want to say seriously
now, I mean I think I've always taken it seriously, but I
give it a lot more weight. ... The need for affordable
housing, to be more efficient with the use of land, a
diminishing resource, all those things I think have made
me change my ideas. (Gregory, interview)

Developers' ideas about why people chose to live in cities paralleled those of the expansionists – access to goods and services – however they talked less explicitly about families or about equity.

What distinguished developers from expansionists was that they were not as intellectually tied to fringe development as a good in itself but only as a means to make money. In a different context, where consolidation was cheaper and where they owned land in existing urban areas, they would consolidate. However, in the context of owning large tracts of land in Rouse Hill they argued that expansion would maintain affordability by increasing the supply of housing. Allied with the expansionists, developers had pushed Rouse Hill along. People from a variety of perspectives referred to the project as "developer driven."

Scientific Environmentalists

Although the Rouse Hill Developement Area owed its genesis to
expansionists and developers, by the 1990s it was being drastically reshaped by environmentalists. Although people in each of
the remaining groups called themselves environmentalists, in this
section I deal with those with a regional, long-term, and "scientific" approach to environmental problems and without a strong
social concern. Part of an expanding group of environmental professionals in both larger environmental organizations and among
bureaucrats, this group relied on highly technical information and
applied science methods.

Scientific environmentalists characterized their position as "holistic," although they had a rather narrow definition of the term with
(ecological) "sustainability [as] the bottom line" (Roger, interview).
As one environmental bureaucrat explained in response to my question about why other groups saw urban development differently:

> *I think the operative word would be sustainability. We're
> not against development by any means, in fact the popu-
> lation has to grow, but really if you're going to do it, do
> it well. It's just what your motivation is, whether it's
> the dollar, whether it's sustainability. And more often
> than not we find now, and I don't know if it's any re-
> flection on Rouse Hill, but the temptation is always there
> for profits, profits, profits. And if you're going to go for
> profits, then your environment is going to suffer. It's
> proportionate, with two extremes. (Roger, interview)*

In Rouse Hill, scientific environmentalists wanted more time to
study and quantify the situation and more time for planning, often
calling for some kind of development moratorium. They believed
they could deal with complicated issues by measuring them accurately. Their central fear was pushing beyond an irreversible limit.
As a representative of the Water Board explained to a conference
on growth in western Sydney:

> *Effective management of any natural resource requires
> multi-objective planning and rational compromise be-
> tween conflicting objectives ... .*
> *To find this balance we have to quantify land degra-
> dation and water quality parameters on the basis of*

*assessments of the river's condition and its anticipated
reaction to development impacts.*

*Until we more fully understand the river system, and
indeed as our understanding increases, the trade-off
between these objectives must never be allowed to push
the ecosystem beyond its ecological limitations – it
would not be able to recover from mismanagement of
this magnitude. Abusing this natural resource beyond
its "environmental threshold" now will leave future generations with a biologically dead river system of no
beauty and little use. (Dodds 1991, n.p.)*

In the face of long-term environmental problems scientific environmentalists tried to argue not only for more study but for new
"baseline" service requirements, new minimum standards for environmental technologies. As an activist explained: "It's either go
the whole hog now, which is terribly expensive, or have no more
urban sprawl in the western Sydney basin, or lose the river system.
They're your choices" (Gerald, interview). In this context they
called for more planning based on a fundamental good, the "yardstick" of environmental protection.

*What we need ... in Sydney is a combined, or a coordi-
nated forward planning land use and urban transport
strategy aimed at improving the water quality in the
Nepean-Hawkesbury system and reducing the levels of
air pollution in the western Sydney basin. Now if forward planning were based on [that], if they were the two
guiding principles of what we did, then we would get
environmentally responsible forward planning. But I think
the Department of Planning should have written into its
credo that we shall do nothing that will increase Sydney's
air pollution or worsen the water quality of the Nepean-
Hawkesbury [River] system, or possibly other rivers as
well. And if suddenly, if everything had to be measured
against that yardstick, you'd have forward planning that
was rational. (Gerald, interview)*

Whether the need to protect the environment was because of
nature's intrinsic worth, because of the effects of ecological damage
on human life, or a combination of the two, was not really important
in this argument. The generally vague level of public debate

obscured these differences often seen as fundamental in scholarly arguments about environmental ethics.

Scientific environmentalists were also comparatively pessimistic about human society. To this group, people were the ones damaging the environment and needed to be controlled to behave responsibly. Although some felt at ease with cities, the majority seemed reluctant converts to the idea of higher densities as a way of physically containing population growth to prevent damaging more natural resources. They supported the approach for strategic reasons, but they did not see much positive value in more dense urban life. Dense cities were more of a technology to mitigate environmental impacts rather than a desirable human environment. As one commented:

> Urban consolidation is an answer and it seems to be the only answer at the moment to cope with the demands for housing. It just has to be planned wisely. I've lived in areas and even worked prior to this job as a volunteer worker at a family crisis-center. That's where they're all putting them into consolidated and densely housed areas. So you create, if you don't have open space et cetera around a development, you create all sorts of social problems. (Roger, interview)

Some scientific environmentalists advocated planning for decentralization to growth areas outside the Sydney region, although in the early 1990s they did not seem to have thought about how to prevent decentralization from merely pushing the same problems somewhere else. Because Sydney was the primary Australian destination for overseas immigrants, others called loudly for a stop to immigration, a call that placed them more or less uneasily on the side of xenophobic opponents of Asian immigration. All warned that continued growth would lead Sydney to become "another Los Angeles," a city of freeways and smog (see chapter three).

In this group's perspective, environmental values were pitted against economic ones with little middle ground. However, as neoclassical economics, dubbed "economic rationalism," was the dominant language of Australian politics they often posed their arguments in terms of a calculation of economic costs and benefits. They supported increased developer charges for infrastructure because they hoped that the high cost would make development of new fringe areas prohibitively expensive. However, privatization moves were not always in their favour as the consortium proposal had, through privatization of physical infrastructure, kept the Rouse Hill project going.

Scientific environmentalists in the bureaucracy also used those environmentalists outside to apply pressure on politicians while they tried to form a sympathetic culture on the inside. Activists mentioned receiving documents leaked by bureaucrats. Bureaucrats, in turn, talked about the pressure put on government by activist arguments. To broaden their base the non-government scientific environmentalists were also often in coalition with local environmentalists in groups such as CHANGE, the Coalition of Hawkesbury and Nepean Groups for the Environment (see next section). Sustainability, in its ecological sense, has been a compelling argument that to date has helped delay future inland growth areas in Sydney, including the later stages of Rouse Hill.

Local Environmentalists

Although for most groups development at Rouse Hill raised a set of regional issues, for local environmentalists Rouse Hill was a threat to their homes and daily activities.

When did I become involved? It was really by accident even though I live very [close]. I have chosen this environment to raise my family because I consider the natural environment and nature very important, and it's one of the philosophies, one of the things I want to be able to give my children.... .

It's the land that the planners seem to look at, not the total picture, not the environment. There's already a community and a lifestyle that exists in the area that's been totally disregarded. And when I've spoken to planners they talked about it as remnant farmland, open fields, and it's really land of little importance. It's land that they see that can be developed, and it's really the opposite of the way I see it. And while [the] people who are making decisions to develop this land are looking at it as, you know, remnant land, they say "subdivide and put houses up." And it's very important land, very important for the sanity of Sydney. It really is the last greenbelt area around Sydney, and when that goes it's

a major threat to the existing urban developments.
(Sarah, interview)

Local environmentalists were among the people most directly
affected by Rouse Hill. Their homes will eventually be surrounded
by it. Often recently arrived, within the last decade or so of exurban
expansion, they were nevertheless committed to the lives they had
made for themselves. This group was very passionate and motivated to save their semi-rural lifestyles.

Closness to "nature" was extremely important to this group,
although their definition of nature was not wilderness untouched
by people, but an aesthetic value, the "unique visual qualities" that
they found when they arrived in the area (Nancy, interview). This
included those "landscape features which have been enjoyed by
artists and people that are tuned in to nature for centuries" (Rufus,
interview).

Although often members of professional households – giving
them a similar background to those employed to work on the
project – their local focus distanced them from those they confronted. They also expressed higher expectations of professionals
than other groups did. In particular, local environmentalists saw
planners as the primary shapers of the urban environment.

> *Whose function is it to keep [natural features] safe for*
> *the rest of the community to enjoy and for the future*
> *community to enjoy? I would suggest it's the responsi-*
> *bility of the town planner. If the town planner has no*
> *awareness or no understanding of these values, then*
> *he will not do his job very well and the community will*
> *suffer over a long period of time. (Rufus, interview)*

Unlike the scientific environmentalists, their relationship with
the bureaucracy was a difficult one. Local environmentalists had
experienced numerous problems with bureaucrats "pass[ing] the
buck" (Rufus, interview). They saw this as due to more than mere
bureaucratic recalcitrance, but rather involving a clash in priorities
among government, consortium, and locals.

> *When you meet with the council, when you meet with*
> *the consortium, when you meet with people from the*
> *government, we sit down, we explain the situation, they*
> *agree with us. But each time we leave they turn to us*

and smile and say, "but we must have housing." So what
we've said and tried to get them to listen to and under-
stand is already dismissed. It's not really being taken
into consideration ... . (Sarah, interview)[6]

In Rouse Hill, local environmentalists had a variety of explanations for this clash in objectives. On the part of planners of various types they saw: a lack of information of the tradeoffs involved in providing housing, a lack of commitment to finding better solutions and gathering adequate data, pressure from the development lobby, bad initial data collection on the corridor that was never rectified, and a predisposition by planners to promote development because their jobs relied on development occurring for them to guide and regulate. As one local environmentalist explained: "When I've spoken to people involved in planning they actually – on a sort of personal level – they agree that they want the best thing for the environment. But that is not in their brief. They have a brief that they've been given. It's usually to develop something, and that's the way they go" (Sarah, interview).

Not all explanations were so generous. Local environmentalists could be very critical of planners and other professionals who did not have detailed local knowledge of the area, or an emotional connection to it, but worked at a broad scale from aerial photographs and selective data sets without visiting the site. One local environmentalist explained: "I realized that the people that ended up in planning jobs in the planning department were basically those who were not bright enough to run a business or have their own expertise accepted in the community" (Rufus, interview). This local environmentalist explained his activism as "a mechanism for grief counseling where people who are affected very badly by government decisions can get with other people who have these affectations,[7] and they can arrive at some sort of balance in their own psyche as to accepting what the government's doing to people" (Rufus, interview). In turn, expansionist and consolidationist planners in state and local government complained about the local environmentalists' confrontational style. This "emotional" and confrontational component also placed them at odds with other landowners (see also Hillier 1993, 105).

The intensely personal impact of Rouse Hill corresponded with local environmentalists' propensities to argue against it in all possible terms:

that they had a right to property, that the council had a responsibility to its rate payers, that professionals were incompetent and evading a clear truth, that everyone deserved clean air and water, that there was a conspiracy that would defraud the public, that the public was unaware and apathetic. With the scientific environmentalists, they warned that Sydney could become "another Los Angeles."

In terms of solutions, they opposed further urban growth. Like the scientific environmentalists, they favored decentralization and halting immigration. Urban consolidation was an inferior option although, as it was often part of their platform in coalitions with scientific environmentalists, local environmentalists were forced to give it quite a bit of attention. They pointed out that consolidation could "be done in an attractive way" and with a "good balance of open space," important components to people who valued visual amenity and natural features highly (Nancy, interview).

However, for this group very low densities were synonymous with a high quality of human existence. When asked why people lived in cities one replied:

> I don't know. I mean I, I haven't lived [in cities], I've lived on the outskirts of cities so it's hard to really understand. And speaking to some people, they seem to think that they need to be surrounded by people. Because I haven't had that environment, haven't grown up in that environment, I don't relate to it, so it's hard for me to relate to that. I just see it as where the infrastructure is, where people have to go. And if there are alternatives, [that's] fantastic, in having smaller centers, are there? Well, is there an alternative? Do we have to have cities? (Nancy, interview)

Although forced, in a similar way, to advocate the use of more public transport, they were both unconvinced about its popularity and, I think, personally not enthusiastic about it. As exurban residents in areas accessible only by car, they had chosen an automobile dependent lifestyle. Although rarely mentioning cars, they were sure that their total lifestyle package was a superior one.

Thus local environmentalists made sense of Rouse Hill as a threat to their good life centered around a particular form of semi-rural family life, in a setting they had worked to acquire. Local environmentalists were, however, only a minority of local residents, if a vocal one. Most residents – from old time farmers to affluent new-comers – wanted development or were at least resigned to it. These residents tried to influence the development's character though formal planning mechanisms, in some cases requesting early development around their homes. In contrast, local environmentalists tried to gain some measure of control over the process through opposition.

Consolidationists

The final group, consolidationists, were generally trained as planners and community workers in the 1970s and 1980s, when spatial inequality, social isolation, and social conflict were high among planning concerns. Although seeing outer suburban growth as inevitable in the very short-term, it was not their favoured long-term option. Rather compact, mixed-use urban forms seemed the most viable way of responding to environmental problems, fiscal austerity, and demographic changes, while maintaining the cultural and social benefits of city life. In answering my question about what Sydney would be like in 20 or 30 years' time, a social planner explained the logic behind her position, but also its unpopularity.

> *It's back to the quarter-acre block thing again. That's OK when you've got your nice little nuclear family. That is not what, or in a few years time that is not what households are going to be made up of. Households are going to be made out of people without children, or elderly people living on their own, and it's totally inappropriate. And most of them wouldn't want to live in a house where they have to look after a garden and they have two spare bedrooms that they never use. So I think there will be a shift in expectations, but it will be fairly slow. I still think there will be a lot of people who think this is their dream, and it's what they're entitled to, and it's what they want. (Margaret, interview)*

Consolidationists also talked about "the other aspect [of their position] being a bit of an environmentalist" (Margaret, interview), something that needed to be balanced with social concerns.

> *I mean I suppose the ideal that I see is that [Sydney will] continue to be a vibrant cultural center, which is what*

cities are, which can minimize the impacts on the natural environment. I think the reality is [that] it's a city environment. It's not a natural environment in any way, and we should be a bit more critical in terms of – it's bit more of a humanist approach – how people can use it better. And presumably if we [value?] some of the range of specifically natural elements, like having a range of fish in our streams, a range of vegetation along those streams and in those areas, [we can figure out] how we can keep those as well. (Andrew, interview)

Through continued suburban expansion consolidationists saw the formation of an environmentally dangerous, socially-divided city where economic and ecological disparities reinforced each other with differential impacts on particular social groups. They were the only group to see urban expansion in terms of social costs; the others focused on social benefits or environmental costs. People who enjoyed suburbs were something of a nuisance to this group who saw themselves as having a more sophisticated view of the public interest.

Consolidationists were also the only professional group I interviewed that included large numbers of women (although women were present as local environmentalists and, to a lesser extent, as scientific environmentalists). Both men and women consolidationists were also more likely than others to refer to experiences working in human services, observing the human costs of suburbs. As a planner working in an environmental bureaucracy explained:

I think that the city unfortunately will increase in its polarization. I think we do have a city of the haves and the have-nots now, and I think that will unfortunately be even more pronounced in the future, which saddens me. And I've actually worked in [outer suburban] places like Parramatta and Campbelltown for about half of my career, and I know what it's like to see people who are a whole lot younger than me pushing prams full of blonde-headed kids up and down the main street and who look obviously shabbily dressed and who you know, you don't know where they've had their last hot meal. I mean I've come into contact with people for whom the

harbor bridge and the opera house are a meaningless
sort of icon. ... I think we run the risk of alienating a
whole lot of people, and we could have some strong
undercurrents and tensions. (Helen, interview)

This offered a particularly striking contrast with expansionists, mostly older and therefore more likely to be men, who talked about planning for nuclear families (like their own), about the egalitarian impact of working-class suburban home ownership, and about its popularity: "I've worked too much in the area, I've worked in the [outer suburbs, the] Mount Druitts and Campbelltowns, there's a place for everybody. I mean people there like it" (Frank, interview, previously quoted).

Like scientific environmentalists, consolidationists talked about the lack of regional coordination. While in theory consolidationists hoped Rouse Hill would be stopped or curtailed, those working on the project had decided to compromise their principles in order to work on it. They reasoned that involvement was better than merely leaving the project to the expansionists and developers. As one explained:

I wanted to see a balance between "lets get it right"
[and stopping the development] because I think it will
still happen no matter what. And I think it's more im-
portant to put energy into ensuring that it happens in
the best possible way rather than putting energy in try-
ing to stop it when your chances are probably fairly
slim. (Margaret, interview)

Consolidationists saw Rouse Hill as partly developer driven and partly inevitable. They hoped, however, that given the increasing social and environmental costs of sprawl, it would be one of the last, large, greenfield developments. Sydney's growth, although dominated at the time by the Department of Housing and the pro-development lobby, could follow a more ecologically, economically, and socially responsible process.

The consolidationists were not very powerful in the early 1990s. Their balancing of multiple objectives seemed weak and naive against more singular perspectives. On the urban fringe their ideas were also pitted against public and private sector developers with high-level government contacts and large financial resources.

Similarities and Differences

The previous section has outlined five ways that groups of professionals, activists, and residents, all middle-class, envisaged urban form in the context of a new suburban development project. In the remainder of the chapter I examine the extent of these similarities and differences among the frameworks; give my interpretation of the importance of roles, interests, and personal experiences in forming these perspectives on urban form; and outline how those involved in Rouse Hill interpreted their differences.

The perspectives in the Rouse Hill debate shared a number of elements. This agreement reflected a common professional background and class position, a common legal and policy context, and a limited historical and geographical situation. In public conferences and reports, and in slightly less public interview and meeting settings, those involved in debating Rouse Hill agreed that free-standing houses were popular; opposition to pollution was increasing in public importance; that privatization was inevitable; and that rational, holistic, or balanced arguments were generally better arguments. Economic language was the dominant language and characteristics that could not be expressed in it were often excluded. Translating infrastructure financing, river ecology, and concepts of community into economic terms involved quite different levels of selection, but did manage to provide a common ground for conversation (see also Nash 1989, 15). Environmental standards formed a secondary language of bottom lines and thresholds. Rouse Hill thus became an area designed to fulfill a quantifiable housing need but with quantifiable environmental impacts, quantifiable financing difficulties, and the potential for quantifiable social problems. This language of quantification, thresholds, and standards was used to describe "air quality," "water quality," and even, through the use of various social indicators, "quality of life" (see Peattie 1987, 126; McCloskey 1985, 141–153 for related analyses).

The one group that sometimes violated these norms of economically rational discussion, the local environmentalists, were widely censured as "hysterical" (Helen, interview). In contrast, those local residents who played by the economically rational rules of development by having their land rezoned, making a speculative profit, and moving out, were both more comprehensible to developers and planners, and far less disturbing.

The perspectives differed, however, in the emphasis they gave environmental and economic issues, how they saw social life, what kinds of urban forms they saw as desirable and practically achievable, and in the content of the arguments they considered to be the most balanced. As these were public debates the concerns for one group had to be at least thought about by others, but they were often treated in different ways and with very different levels of seriousness or coherence. The result was a pattern of converging and diverging visions that both enabled strategic alliances and provoked conflicts, and could not be reduced to two sides.

Both expansionists and developers saw growth as inevitable, wanted housing to be affordable to the majority of the middle and working classes, and saw environmental concerns as overstated and needlessly expensive to confront. Expansionists, however, were stubbornly committed to suburbia as a good end in itself, a social benefit in terms of the character of environment and the access to opportunities and services it provided. In contrast, developers could support a variety of urban forms while still making profits and building things. They were also generally less vocal. Developers had access to capital and high-level government contacts and so the persuasive power of their ideas – at least to more general audiences – was less important. For others, compelling perspectives or stories were vital in that the persuasive, legitimating, and rationalizing power of ideas was a major form of power (Marris 1990).

While the various environmentalists saw the need for limits, their specific concerns were quite different. For scientific environmentalists, consolidation was a means toward an end of minimizing ecological damage to the Sydney region. Social issues did not figure in their perspective except in terms of figuring out how to control environmentally damaging human actions. For local environmentalists, consolidation was a necessary, if unattractive, means of protecting their local environment. For consolidationists, in contrast, compact urban forms had a wider set of social and cultural benefits, benefits that other groups either did not see or more actively questioned.

The positions had a complicated relationship with the positions of formal political parties. A consensus about the benefits of growth in the immediate postwar period had been replaced by the 1990s with a concern about the various costs of growth. By the early

1990s the state Liberal-National government and the federal Labor government agreed that growth had severe costs. As I have shown, however, those involved with the development, and in the wider debates, disagreed on whether and which of these costs were excessive. Even cabinet members within the same government took opposing positions. The departments they oversaw were often internally divided in terms of views on growth.

These perspectives on good city form did not necessarily involve images of streets and houses. The form of the city was seen as collection of elements that could be bought and sold, the context for access to social and cultural opportunities, a means of promoting social equality, a source of social division, or a technology with measurable environmental impacts. Perspectives also reflected the practical constraints of implementation, what these middle-level professionals and activist leaders thought they had the power to do or to influence. In more reflective moments some could imagine a number of possible options for urban development, but practically they focused on the proposals they thought the best that could be achieved.

As I proposed in chapter one, the perspectives or frameworks were related to roles or interests: expansionists, many scientific environmentalists, and consolidationists were involved in the project professionally; developers and local environmentalists were local landowners or employees of landowners. However, people with the same function, with similar experiences and interests, who had chosen to work in similar jobs in the same agencies, who had moved to the Rouse Hill area at about the same time, had different perspectives on urban growth. Thus a level of interpretation was occuring in the translation of interests into an image of good city form.[8]

One explanation for these interpretive differences between the frameworks that coexisted in the early 1990s is that they reflected a kind of generational effect as described by Mannheim (1952; Ginsburg 1989, 139–140; Burner 1986, 139).[9] To Mannheim, generations are structured in a similar way to class positions, limiting individuals "to a specific range of potential experience, predisposing them for a characteristic mode of thought and experience, and a characteristic type of historically relevent action" (1952, 291). Certain experiences are fresh in each new generation and have great impact. Older generations have already developed "framework[s] of usable past experience" (296) that they can slot these new experiences into without much change to their perspective. It is the younger cohorts that are most deeply affected by change. The length of generations thus varies with the pace of change. Members of one generation who differ in the way they "work up" their experiences into frameworks comprise different "generation units" (304). Rouse Hill's lengthy planning and development process meant that several generations and generation units was involved, particularly reflected in diverging views on family life and the natural environment.[10]

People were explicit about the experiential basis of their ideas. In answering a question about how their ideas about suburban growth were formed, over half of those interviewed talked first about their own housing history as the main experience shaping their ideas. Most of the rest came up with anecdotes from professional work or travel. In interview after interview informants talked about their childhood, early years of marriage, and the beginning of their careers, as key in shaping their approach to growth. These experiences were quite different for two key groups. First were those coming to adulthood in the early postwar years, who had formed nuclear families, had helped develop the middle and early outer ring of suburbs, and at the time of the interviews were aged in their late 50s and 60s. The second group were those reaching adulthood in the 1970s and early 1980s once the costs of growth were apparent and at a time when the best development areas had largerly been used up. This generational effect was important for expansionists, consolidationsts, and scientific environmentalists, with the logic of property ownership stronger among the other groups.

Overlaid upon these generational effects and housing histories were a set of assumptions about class and gender. Expansionists, more often older men, talked about planning for nuclear families (like their own), the egalitarian character of working-class suburban home ownership, and the popularity of suburbs: "people there like it" (Frank, previously quoted). Consolidationists, often younger, involved in human services, and more likely to be women, noticed "people who are a whole lot younger than me pushing prams full of blonde-headed kids up and down the main street and who look obviously shabbily dressed and who, you know, you don't know where they've had their last hot meal"(Helen, interview, previously quoted).

The following quotes from interviews evoke some of the use of personal experience in formulating ideas about suburbs and suburban development:

> Ann: Where were your ideas formed about suburbia?
> Alan (consolidationist, late 20s to early 30s): Probably my childhood in Canberra. Because I lived in a Radburn scheme.... . I never had to cross a road, I was always basically in a park, I was never very far from anything, and nothing bad used to happen. Everything was just fine, nice trees, grass. Everything was good.... .
>
> I also found when I got a car it was fantastic thing to drive in Canberra because there was no congestion, but you still took a really long time to get from one place to another because it was so spread out and the density was so low and every center was separated by either topographic or physical barriers.... . [So] traveling time is ridiculous and you're just burning petrol the whole time and it's car-based and all those problems started to just weigh on me.
>
> Ann: [Can you tell me] how your ideas about suburban development, perhaps getting back to human services, were formed?
> Margaret (consolidationist, 40s): I suppose one of the things is I lived in [an affluent outer suburb] and that probably did have a major impact. I migrated here when my children were little, so I actually lived in a new housing area... and certainly that can have a detrimental effect on your whole life.
>
> Ann: What formed your ideas about suburbia?
> Frank (expansionist, mid 50s to early 60s): Yeah, my views of suburbia? I mean I have views. I love living in inner suburbs and things. In fact from the age of eight to 28 I lived in a small flat in [a harbor-side suburb], which is, you know these Bondi-type [three-story] flats. And so it's not as if I've got a hang-up about living in flats and [think everyone] should move to suburbia, not at all. In fact my theory is children love high density. It's the parents who hate it, the parents can't stand it because of the noise and the kids love it because there's lots of kids around. It's wonderful.

*But it's parents who, whenever they could afford it,
got out of that [and although they] said "the back yard's
for the children," it wasn't for the children at all. It was
for them, and you can understand that.*

In spite of these differences, however, in each case ideas about
the social world of the city – although differing – shared a characteristic I call "thinness".[11] That is, they did not envisage society as
rich networks of multiple interdependencies. For expansionists it
was a world of private male-headed families where an essentially
dislocated family unit ventured out into the world to gain access to
economic and cultural opportunities. This image of economic men
formed part of the basis of their alliance with developers. A larger
human society as a positive whole was at most conceptualized as a
market, buying and selling things that were created by individuals
and corporations, rather than as a more multifaceted setting for
diverse human relations.

Scientific environmentalists probably shared some of this economic view of the city, but it was secondary to their main concern
and that was the destructive force of human society. They were
negative or ambivalent about the collective life of the city. Humans were essentially damaging and dangerous. Meanwhile local
environmentalists seemed to split the social world into two groups:
those, like themselves, attuned to nature; and those who lived in
urban areas huddling close to infrastructure in an inferior lifestyle.
These were problematic catagories as local environmentalists hardly
wanted a great conversion of people to their way of life, potentially crowding them out (see also Dorst 1989, 22). However, I am
not sure that local environmentalists saw this potential paradox
clearly.

Even the consolidationists, who conceived of a demographi-
cally more diverse society and talked about the negative possibilities of social isolation and social conflict, described society
more as a set of social issues than social networks. It could be
that these stronger attachments were so intrinsic to people's lives
that they did not think to articulate them, but perhaps it also reflects the ways that economic or ecological terms began to shape
the ways people saw themselves rather than merely limit the ways
they expressed ideas (c.f. Bellah *et al.* 1985, 8).

I was surprised by the lack of a rich view of contemporary social life. Trained as an urban planner in the social science tradition, I was strongly influenced by discussions about the character of community, justice, and social change. From numerous positions – modernist, postcolonial, communitarian – recent debates in these areas have been grappling with issues such as people's obligations to one another and the character of group identity. This obsession with ideas about social life turned out to be unusual in the professional and activist debates. I need not have been so surprised about this, however. Two Australian studies, recently completed at the time of my fieldwork, described similar thin conceptions of society in groups that frame the middle-class, middle-level professionals and activists I studied.

Pusey's (1991) *Economic Rationalism in Canberra* was based on a survey of 215 members of the Senior Executive Service, the elite bureaucrats in the Australian federal government, which was Labor at the time. He found that although this group were relatively confident in talking about the economy, they had difficulty in talking about society except as a series of issues or problems (Pusey 1991, 41). In a very different social context Richards, in a longitudinal study of residents moving into and living in a new outer suburb in Melbourne, found people valued the physical space of the house rather than the social space of the neighborhood (Richards 1990, 11–12). This replicated previous findings in the US and Canada, and in Sydney.[12]

Whether the lack of depth in public positions in Rouse Hill was due to problems in articulation, or reflected a profound absence, it nevertheless formed a powerful context for debates over growth (see Perin 1988, 63–106; Biellah *et al.* 1985). Pusey's work on bureaucrats had wider press coverage, but each study was mentioned to me several times in the course of my fieldwork by people using the findings to interpret or confirm their experiences.

Participants' Observations of Difference

These are my analyses of the situation, reflecting my insider-outsider status and my research approach. Those involved in Rouse Hill had their own opinions both about the character of differences among perspectives, and about the reasons for these differences.

The range of responses was shown when answering my question about why other people saw things differently. For some the question was surprising, and perhaps even unimportant.

> *That's a good question, I dont't know, I don't know.*
> *[laugh] I really can't answer that. I don't know the*
> *answer. (Timothy, developer, interview).*

Others had a more traditional interest-based explanation with the interests of public and private sector developers confronting the interests of others wanting to reshape the development.

> *There's a number of factors there. I think one of the*
> *main factors is self interest... the pace and approach of*
> *the proposal ... I think was very threatening to the*
> *established way of doing things. ... The whole private*
> *sector participation ... these horrible money making*
> *people who are trying to screw us to the wall and pro-*
> *vide no facilities and just simply get away with as much*
> *profit as they can. (Gregory, developer, interview)*

> *There are others who have very powerful vested inter-*
> *est reasons for [growth]. (Gerald, scientific environ-*
> *mentalist, interview)*

> *And you're fighting some very strong interests, the inter-*
> *ests of developers who find that greenfield sites are just*
> *easier and cheaper to develop. In many ways they are,*
> *and once again Sydney would grow. (Andrew, consoli-*
> *dationist, interview)*

A significant group pointed to issues of knowledge and understanding, assuming that if people shared the same knowledge or information that they would come to the same conclusions.

> *OK. I'm not, it's very difficult. I find that a very difficult*
> *question to answer. I think a lot of people don't have a*
> *very good understanding of housing issues in Sydney ... .*
> *(Helen, consolidationist, interview)*

> *The level of knowledge that's around that's shared by*
> *everyone is not high. (George, intellectual, interview)*

> *Maybe they're naive. I think more so it's probably po-*
> *litical naiveté. (Dennis, local speculator, interview)*

Still others pointed to subjectively-held basic values, related to experiences and to interests but also to what was in people's "hearts." This affected the kind of commitment individuals brought to their work and activism.

> *There's a whole range of arguments you can follow through and they're all quite logical and what you come back to is a subjective first premise, always a subjective first premise. ... And I mean the people who are brought up by sort of millionaire developers to rape and pillage, their fundamental moral principles are based on a belief that its right to do that, and that it's necessary, and that it's a valuable thing to do it. (Gerald, scientific environmentalist, interview, see also MacIntyre 1981,8)*

> *It all breaks down to values, doesn't it?... Well the community has vision, as I said, and their hearts in it. It's not [like that for everyone] as I was saying of the bureaucrats, it's a nine to five job ... . The developers see it as a way of getting a return and [are] not really looking at the long-term impacts they're creating on the environment. They're looking at it in the short-term and not the long-term, and it is biased... . (Nancy, local environmentalist, interview)*

Thus participants explained their own differences in several ways, as: totally inexplicable; due to different interests; caused by different amounts of knowledge; due to resentment about change, particularly privatization; and resulting from differences in premises or values where this was due to people starting with the wrong first premises or because first premises are never more than subjective. These explanations represent quite a range of interpretations. Some people implied that with equal amounts of knowledge people could agree. Others thought interests, or fundamental values, divided people.

There did not seem to be a narrow correspondence between perspectives on urban form and explanations of differences. Environmentalists, particularly local environmentalists, did talk more about values, but they also discussed the interests of developers and politicians. Others mentioned differences in knowledge more often, while also referring to interests. These were only broad tendencies, contradicted in many instances.

Perhaps this level of incoherence – at least relative to the five frameworks – reflects a lack of public debate about why people saw things differently. Perspectives on urban form were a hot topic in Sydney's environmental and planning circles in the early 1990s and people involved in the issues had, at some time, to place themselves in the debate. The level of discussion provided a great deal of information from which to choose; and the controversy forced positions to become more coherent and defensible. Similarly people, in order to act, had to have some ideas about power relations and about their own sources of power. However, a deep understanding about why people saw things differently – except insofar as it was necessary for political strategies such as changing values – was just not as necessary. It did not seem to particularly trouble people that others saw things so differently, except to the extent that it thwarted their purposes. That they were more right and others less so was an ordinary situation needing only fairly simple explanations.

While some characteristics were defining features of groups and were shared by all members – a focus on providing family housing for expansionists, a commitment to ecological sustainability for scientific environmentalists – on less central issues people within groups could vary significantly in their opinions. Developers, for instance, gave a variety of reasons for why people lived in cities. Local environmentalists had differing perspectives on affordable housing with some seeing it as an important issue to tackle and others not. Frameworks had areas of variation as well as certain core features.

Although incorporating many simplifications and stereotypes, perspectives did represent a compelling and workable vision formed through long experience, in response to the important issues of the time, and in the context of differing power resources (see Majone 1989, 32). This is not to say people were completely locked into one path, but neither did they change ideas easily. People were often deeply suspicious of each other and harshly dismissive of others' views and strategies. They rarely met each other in forums that promoted free-ranging discussion of issues, and they did not express much interest in doing so.[13] A few groups were sure that once I understood their side I could act as a kind of independent expert witness, arguing for their cause and undermining others.

These reflections do not exhaust the possible areas of commonality and difference in the various positions. Moreover, most professionals, while holding particular ideas about urban form, could step back from these at times to a more purely administrative or technical role leaving larger decisions to the formal political process. Even activists had varying levels of commitment to their ideas in different situations. Thus along with qualitative differences in perspective were quantitative differences in commitment or passion. Overall these frameworks describe the range of most vocal opinion on Rouse Hill and are common perspectives elsewhere. In the next chapter I explore in more depth some ways the groups represented these positions.

End Notes

[1] In what is otherwise a quite subtle analysis of the complexity of interests, Schwarz and Thompson (1990,124) use this kind of formulation; for example, writing of "civil engineers" as a unified group. Elsewhere they propose a more generic, four part, typology of rationalities: the fatalist, hierarchist, individualist, and egalitarian (for professional training classifications see also Calavita and Caves 1994; Marris 1987; Peattie 1987; Schneider 1989).

[2] Some informants came up with well developed classifications that paralleled my own analysis. Others did not contradict these typologies but tended to collapse together groups they were not familiar with, such as "environmentalists" or "bureaucrats." The categories of consolidationists and expansionists, both mainly involving planners and other bureaucrats, were the least well articulated.

[3] Whether or not this characterization of working-class home ownership was entirely true was another matter.

[4] Expansionists in Sydney, however, were not pure followers of Stretton, as he was somewhat negative about Sydney (Stretton 1989, 274).

[5] The Australian figure includes households with additional adults as well (Castles 1994, 100–101).

[6] Sarah's descriptions of this conversation echoes a 1946 broadcast by novelist E.M. Forster who had lived in the area of Stevenage and was unhappy about proposals for a new town: " "well", says the voice of planning and progress, "why this sentimentality? People must have houses" " (quoted in Orlans 1953,142).

[7] Rufus probably meant to say people who were "affected" (by the development). Interestingly, affected means both "influenced injuriously," which he thought he had been, and also something which is "assumed artificially," which was an accusation leveled at local environmentalists about their environmentalism (*Concise Macquarie Dictionary*).

[8] This study of perspectives drew on previous work on normative theories of urban form. Lynch (1981, chapter 4) describes three such theories: representing a cosmic order, as a practical machine, and as an organism. Peattie (1987, 44–45), in her analysis of planning Ciudad Guayana, describes five ways to think of a city, as: "built form – building, open spaces, passages, barriers"; "a system of rules and regulations –taxes, building codes, rules of ownership and tenancy"; "social relationships and social institutions – neighborhoods, organizations, ethnic groupings"; "an arena of power and of the political arrangements which organize power"; and "an economic system – capital investment, supplies of labor, housing and land markets". In related work Meinig (1979) describes, from a geographical perspective, ten ways of reading a landscape, as: nature with people removed, a habitat for people, an artifact of human creation, a system (a scientific view), a problem needing social action, wealth, representing an ideology, history, place, and in aesthetic terms. At a more general level, perspectives also resemble Schon and Rein's (1994, vii) institutional action frames and metacultural frames.

[9] Although Mannheim's work is now dated, his hypothesis of generational effects on memory and attitude has been confirmed in recent open-ended survey research (Schuman and Scott 1989; Swidler and Arditi 1994, 301).

[10] The generational shifts were reinforced by the world of work. With the rise of (the perception of) environmental problems and financial concerns, jobs expanded for environmental bureaucrats and economists even as jobs serving social issues declined. Thus, in the 1990s, more people were paid to think about economic and environmental concerns and this was at least partly reflected in debates. In these areas humans were conceptualized as interacting through markets and as damaging natural resources. Those that were paid to deal with social issues were both relatively powerless and focused on the negative side of social life, on social problems. By the 1990s the character of Australian cities had also shifted, generally becoming physically larger and perhaps more unequal. This administrative history formed part of the context for the experiences, and interpretations of those experiences, people drew upon when debating Rouse Hill.

[11] This was inspired by Geertz (1973, 6) who was in turn inspired by Gilbert Ryle.

[12] Classic North American studies include Clark (1996) and Gans (1967). The Cumberland County Council (1948, 104) noted similar thin ideas. Troy (1971, 1), in a study in Sydney, claimed that people did value a variety of social elements, but his examples seemed to indicate the opposite.

[13] Schwarz and Thompson (1990) make a similar argument about persistent disagreement among experts in science and technology fields.

CHAPTER THREE

Visual Rhetorics in Growth Debates: Sydney's Future as a Los Angeles, Toronto, or Canberra

In disputes over urban development, such as the one over Rouse Hill, arguments frequently hinge not on what is, but on what could be. This chapter explores a class of images that were used in the Rouse Hill project and are frequently used in planning and growth debates; describing the future of an urban development with the name or picture of another place. This form of synecdoche and metaphor taps into cultural and subcultural understandings of other places, with these understandings shaped at least in part by media images. This a common politics in urban development and urban design as people try to understand, explain and persuade; verbally or visually evoking Manhattan, Paris, Beirut, Hong Kong, or Disneyland as an image of the future (e.g. Peattie 1991, 36).

In the early 1990s, in meetings and interviews, reports and newsletters, newspaper and television accounts, three such images provided an intriguing way of imagining the future of Rouse Hill and of Sydney. Although the various environmental professionals and activists criticizing inland expansion were split on a number of issues, they all managed to agree that, without firm intervention, Sydney would become "another Los Angeles." However, some pointed to an alternative path away from automobile dependence like the one that "European" Toronto had followed. For another group, particularly expansionist planners, the contrasting image of "doing a Canberra" evoked both the possibility of creating a utopian city in the growth corridor, but also provided a warning about the huge investment that entailed.

Of the groups actually involved in debates about the development, only the development professionals had relatively consistent and direct access to such power bases as the state cabinet and large lending institutions; the kind of political, economic, and institutional power that could shape the development directly. Others had more need to shape public opinion and professional consciousness to value certain urban forms. The city images I discuss were a key mechanism for reaching out both to other professionals and to wider publics in the early 1990s. The expansionist planners were most likely to evoke a positive image of the corridor as "doing a Canberra"; the consolidationist planners to use the image as a warning of the need for resources. The environmentalists focused on regional and local issues warned about forming "another Los Angeles."

Returning to this study area in the mid-1990s, with the first houses in the growth corridor already occupied, the city comparisons were no longer in as much currency. While in vogue, however, these were powerful and accessible images evoking other suburban-type cities through their names, short descriptions, and carefully chosen slides. The images related highly technical arguments through pictures of desirable or frightening futures. For those groups lacking easy access to institutional and political power, compelling arguments based in these accessible images were important means of influence.

The city images were so popular that "discovering" them did not involve much sifting work. Interpreting their meaning, however, engaged me in a more subtle hermeneutic circle. Unlike many of those participating in the Sydney discussions, I also had first hand experiences of all the cities mentioned in the debates, including experience as a resident of Los Angeles. Although the chapter relies on data from documents, interviews, and meetings in developing its argument, this personal background gave me an insider-outsider status that was extremely useful in the research (Greenhouse 1985). This made me particularly sensitive when, for example, "Los Angeles" sometimes meant "smog" and sometimes meant "sprawl," but rarely meant the kind of complex metropolitan region that I had lived in for two years.[1]

As I examined the growth debates I became intrigued with how the widespread practice of using an image of another named city to represent an urban development's future shaped the kinds of actions that could be imagined. What did these images highlight and what was obscured, silenced, or even misrepresented? Two kinds of rhetorical devices seemed particularly important. Most obvious were metaphors where a word is applied to something to which it is not literally applicable: a fringe suburban growth corridor as a new city like Canberra. More interestingly, these images were a form of very visual and regionally-shaped synecdoche, a figure of speech where a whole is named but a part understood (Los Angeles standing for smog), or a part is named but a whole understood (Los Angeles standing for all of the US).

In these particular city images parts and wholes were linked in a complex web of meaning. Crucially, the images were truer to professionals' and activists' hopes and fears for the future than to the details of the situation in Sydney, Canberra, Los Angeles, or Toronto. The images tapped into a set of cultural understandings or imaginings partly formed by the mainstream visual media, partly by planning lore, and partly through the debates themselves. These images of possible futures created scenarios that left room for the professionals and activists who used them to have a role protecting and shaping the environment. These characteristics of multiple meanings, visual emphasis, regional flavor, misrepresentation of details, and professional empowerment provide the focus for the final part of the chapter.

"ANOTHER LOS ANGELES" AND A " 'EUROPEAN' TORONTO"

Image Structure and Context

While including some areas for commercial and industrial development, and described as a "new city," the Rouse Hill growth corridor was proposed in the late 1960s as a development primarily meeting the expected demand for suburban housing (SPA 1968, 22). This made transport for residents to workplaces outside the area a key issue. While a railway line ran through the area, adjacent flood lands severely limited development potential near the line. From the start of detailed planning, buses on ordinary roads were seen as the major form of public transport (Pund and Fleming 1997). It was generally agreed that private transport – cars – would play a key role. Throughout the corridor's planning this caused concern as the area was serviced primarily by rural roads and upgrading would be expensive.

Set on a costal plain and surrounded by mountains, Sydney experiences air inversion effects. From the corridor's early detailed planning in the 1980s, air pollution emerged as a problem, although only in the 1990s was it characterized as excessively severe and amenable to control through growth limits. In this latter period, two events catalyzed political action over air pollution: high smog levels in May 1991, dubbed the "smog event"; and the release after Freedom of Information requests of a 1990 study on air quality (Hyde and Johnson 1990).

That study, sponsored as part of the investigation of two additional southern inland growth sectors, found air pollution had declined close to the coast. It had, however, increased inland due to changes in the composition of vehicle exhausts following the introduction of catalytic converters. Pollution had shifted inland (downwind) and was likely to increase dramatically with urban growth. Most importantly, the Rouse Hill Development Area was sited exactly in the location where most of Sydney's pollution pooled overnight in calm periods. Even if the residents in the area lived car-free lives they would still experience high pollution level (Hyde and Johnson 1990, 1–7; Johnson 1991).

Local and scientific environmentalists pointed out that Sydney, with its inversion effects, was becoming "another Los Angeles" and the inland development would exacerbate this. As Dr. David Hughes, a physician who was president of the large Coalition of Hawkesbury and Nepean Groups for the Environment (CHANGE), explained:

> *Faced with the realisation that the urban dream is often a myth, residents of Western Sydney now find that their environmental amenity is being threatened even more, by Sydney's landuse and urban transport strategies. Dependence upon the private motor vehicle in Greater Sydney, and a failure to really address the issue or rail options for public transport, are leading to serious issues of air pollution for residents who are often forced, for economic reasons, to live in the Nepean-Hawkesbury Basin. The CSIRO-Macquarie University Pilot Study [Hyde and Johnson 1990] into air quality has found that on some days, air pollution is more than double acceptable public health limits in parts of the region... .*

*What we are doing, knowingly, is allowing the de-
velopment of another Los Angeles in the West of Sydney.
(Hughes 1991, 7)*

The image of "another Los Angeles," popularized by Dr. Hughes and others, was used in written materials, in speeches, and taken up by newspapers, radio, and television (e.g. Allison 1991a; Earthworm 1991; Finlay 1994; Travers 1991; Trembath 1991).[2] However, as well as drawing on popular knowledge and on the Hyde and Johnson study, people using this metaphor also evoked the work of perth academics, Peter Newman and Jeff Kenworthy.

During the early 1990s, following the publication of their book on *Cities and Automobile Dependence* (1989a), Newman and Kenworthy traveled to Sydney regularly to give lectures to professional and community groups. Their book was not in wide circulation; at around 150 Australian dollars it was beyond the price range of many professionals. Their research focusing on the links between urban form and car use was, however, widely known through their frequent lectures and a number of shorter journal publications. The expense of the book became important for the debate as it meant few of those listening to the oral presentations had easy access to the book to check the detailed findings laid out in lengthy appendices, particularly in the first few years after the book's publication.

Newman and Kenworthy had personally collected data on land use and transportation from 32 major cities in Europe, North America, Australia, and Asia for 1960, 1970, and 1980. From these data they argued that although incomes, fuel efficiency, and oil prices accounted for 40 to 50 percent of gasoline use in major world cities (and by implication air pollution), the physical form of cities was also an important variable (Newman and Kenworthy 1989a, 73). Residential and employment density, road length per capita and per vehicle, numbers of cars and car parking spaces, provision of public transit, and job distribution, although not city size, explained much of the remaining geographical variation in automobile, and thus gasoline, use.[3] Of particular interest was a finding that cities, or parts of cities, where significant proportions of the population used public transport rather than automobiles had densities over 30 or 40 persons per hectare (Newman and Kenworthy 1989a, 127–129).

Newman and Kenworthy's Sydney presentations emphasized the roles of planners in manipulating urban form to reduce gasoline use, particularly in terms of the measurable variables of population or housing density, and road length per capita. A graph of density versus energy use was a prominent part of their talks and was widely reproduced (Newman and Kenworthy 1989a, figure 5.7; Bailey 1991). The density versus energy use chart showed a sweeping black curved line joining, but also separating, European and Asian cities with high density and low energy use and US cities with the opposite.

In their presentations Newman and Kenworthy juxtaposed aerial slides of the Los Angeles freeway system under a dirty smog haze with closer up views of high-density, mixed-use, urban village type developments around transit nodes in Europe and Toronto (Kenworthy 1991b; Newman 1991). As Kenworthy wrote at about the same time: "Australian cities have the opportunity to learn from Toronto's vision and approach to urban development. The alternative appears to be a gradual drift towards the Los Angeles model with all the problems this entails" (Kenworthy 1991a, 154).

The Images' Shortfalls

The images of Los Angeles and Toronto were thus quite graphically presented in Sydney by experts such as Newman and Kenworthy and more widely publicized by activists through the media.[4] However, the focus on Toronto and Los Angeles as the alternative possibilities for the future development of Sydney was misleading, especially given its basis in the Newman and Kenworthy study of physical characteristics of these cities focused on density and road length. In 1980, the latest figures in Newman and Kenworthy's book, Sydney was slightly *less* dense than LA and it had a *greater* length of road per capita (see table 1).[5] Thus in terms of the two variables emphasized in public speeches by Newman and Kenworthy as leading inexorably to high automobile use, Sydney was already in worse shape than Los Angeles. Yet in Sydney people drove much less each year and each took many more transit trips, even when adjusted for incomes and prices. Newman and Kenworthy did not mention the actual densities of Los Angeles and Sydney in the presentations I attended. In contrast, high-density Toronto, Newman and Kenworthy's public transport utopia in

TABLE 1
NEWMAN AND KENWORTHY'S SYDNEY, LOS ANGELES, AND
TORONTO FIGURES, 1980

	Sydney	Los Angeles	Toronto
Gross Density (Persons/ha)	17.6	20.0	39.6
Road Length per Capita (Meters)	6.2	4.5	2.7
Passenger (?) Vehicle Kilometers per Year	6,442	10,003	7,422
Transit Trips per Capita per Year	142.3	59.2	177.6

Source: *Newman and Kenworthy (1989a, 317–318, 339–340, 343–344).*

their Sydney presentations, had just a little more transit use than Sydney but also more travel by car.[6]

Thus Los Angeles and Toronto were not the best cities to compare with Sydney to illustrate that low-densities and longer lengths of road per capita led to auto-dependence and that higher densities decreased it. The paired comparisons of LA-Sydney and Sydney-Toronto actually "proved" the exact opposite. For Toronto, Los Angeles, and Sydney other variables such as the number of car spaces per-CBD worker showed a clearer pattern, as did their historical development, but Newman and Kenworthy did not emphasize these variables in lectures.

Although there is heated disagreement about how to measure city densities, in terms of the data presented in their own book their comparison was misplaced. For the particular variables they chose to emphasize, it would have been far more precise for Newman and Kenworthy to say Sydney could deteriorate into another Perth or Phoenix or even San Francisco's metropolitan area (all metropolitan areas less dense than Sydney), or in contrast take the path of Singapore or Paris or Moscow away from automobile dependence.

However, the images of "another Los Angeles" and a "European" Toronto were not simply about presenting data. Rather they were a strategic use of cultural symbols.

Perth and Phoenix just did not carry the negative symbolic weight
of smoggy, sprawling, superficial, materialistic LA. Moreover,
many Australians had come as immigrants to get away from Asian
and European cities, and others had visited them and been happy
to return to suburban Sydney. Thus proposing a European or Asian
alternative was unlikely to be as attractive as the relatively un-
known Commonwealth Toronto, part of a country perceived to be
culturally similar to Australia and looked on approvingly in
planning circles (e.g. SPA 1968, 43; c.f. Kenworthy 1991a, 148,
153). Thus the images Newman and Kenworthy chose reflected
the general thrust of their research, while obscuring its detailed
findings. They were indeed talking about Sydney becoming "another Los Angeles" in the sense of a Los Angeles somewhat different to the Los Angeles described in their book.

Newman and Kenworthy's presentations reinforced negative
views of Los Angeles and, with popular interpretations of the Hyde
and Johnson study, gave a stamp of expert or scientific approval to
activists' warnings of a Los Angeles-style future. As one local environmental activist claimed:

> And it becomes the same situation as Los Angeles which
> has been shown historically and at present to be a di-
> saster. And any person who studies town planning, any
> person who studies architecture, knows that [the] Los
> Angeles style [of] planning and urban sprawl are things
> that are very bad and yet we have the Department of
> Planning that is perpetrating exactly this style of plan-
> ning. (Rufus, interview)

For those who saw Los Angeles as a frightening dystopia,
the original proposal of development of the Rouse Hill growth
corridor seemed quite irrational and it was often interpreted
as a regrettable mistake. This hypothesis of ignorance was, however, only partially true as even the earliest detailed planning
documents in the 1980s had noted severe air pollution problems
while recommending the corridor go forward (DEP 1982, 18;
1984a, 80, 84). In interviews pro-expansion planners and developers from a variety of planning and housing agencies often described
Los Angeles in a more benign way. These groups that had laid
the planning structure for the Rouse Hill, argued that Los Angeles

did not "choke to death," that mobility was a positive thing, and that technological changes could eliminate any danger (Frank, interview).

"DOING A CANBERRA"

Image Structure and Context

Los Angeles and Toronto formed images for the future of all of Sydney as well as the growth corridor. However, they were not the only cities with which the development was compared. Its various development concepts, with populations projected generally in excess of 250,000, evoked a steady stream of comparisons with the Australian national capital, Canberra. Planners and others used these comparisons to help politicians and the wider public visualize the scale of the undertaking. As one expansionist planner explained:

> People have got to understand the scale of what we're talking about, we're talking about a Canberra. We made that [comparison], I think you'll see that in the first area of 250,000, to show people what we're talking about, we're talking about a Canberra. And you can't just put those people elsewhere because if you look at Canberra, Canberra started in 1911[7] and its only just reached 270,000 with all the money that the Commonwealth had at its disposal. And its done extremely well, [but] you just can't have lots of [new cities]. And to start off a new city somewhere is even more expensive than starting off [Rouse Hill]. At least you can get the water from Prospect [reservoir]. At least there's billions of dollars spent on the whole water catchment area [and] you've just got to tap that. While it's expensive [to build the corridor], to start a whole new city is ridiculous. (Frank, interview)

This focus on Canberra was not inevitable: people could have compared the Rouse Hill corridor with Newcastle or Wollongong, similar sized steel-producing cities to the north and south of Sydney. In 1986 Newcastle's population was 256,000, Canberra's 247,000, and Wollongong's 207,000, making them the sixth, seventh, and eighth largest Australian cities respectively (Castles 1988, 4).

However, people rarely used these other cities as comparisons. Although often explicitly about size, the underlying theme of the Canberra image was about financial and intellectual resources, particularly the government resources that Canberra had lots of and the other cities few. Two passages from the *Sydney Morning Herald*, one from its Northern Suburbs supplement, make this clear.

> *When the [state] Premier, Mr. Greiner, annouced plans for a new mini city in the north-western suburbs of Sydney, he said it would be "like building another city the size of Canberra."*
>
> *But will it get the same financial backing that Canberra has had? (Boson 1989, 4)*

> *Dr. Hughes [from CHANGE] said a city the size of Canberra was being dumped on a bankrupt Baulkham Hills Shire, which would take the blame from the State Government for inadequate roads and transport. (Allison 1991b, 6)*

These references to Canberra evoked other aspects of Canberra as well: suburban, green, automobile dependent (see also Logan 1992, 5; RHCPT 1992b, 5; Riddell 1991; WSROC 1984,2). These aspects were not unambiguously good or bad and so the image was a contradictory one. For groups like the expansionist planners, car-based environments, whatever their drawbacks, gave an appealing form of automobility to large groups of people. For others, including many scientific environmentalists, automobile dependence was a disaster.

Although the various accounts pointed to the high level of resources Canberra had received, this did not necessarily mean that all involved wanted the same subsidies for the Rouse Hill development. Some may have, but others were highlighting the difficulty of developing such a large site in a period and a place where extensive government investments were unlikely. For those concerned with social services it was obvious that: "An area the size of Canberra needs more than one youth worker de-funded [the outer suburban Local Government Area of] Liverpool" (Arnold, meeting transcript). However, it was quite possible that this was the kind of social service provision the corridor would get, at least in the initial stages.

In addition, for some planners working on the project, the image of Canberra also evoked a more personally compelling reason for involvement in the corridor that, while still about scale and resources, had a more exciting gloss. The opportunity to "do a Canberra" allowed planners to build a new "mini city" (Boson 1989). It was a chance to leave one's mark, to create something new, to do things better than one could in more fragmented projects. Reflecting on the lot of local government planners, a senior expansionist planner summarized this appeal.

> *With planning there's so many subjective opinions. There's always controversy over it, always room for debate. And you find that it's always the thing that creates the most activity at council, verbal activity that is, and of course puts a lot of pressure on planners. And a lot them opt out rather than put up with it because may be it's not too bad outside there or in the state government where you've only got to convince one person or so. But here you've got a stack of aldermen all with different ideas and it really sends you up the wall.*
>
> *And so we don't have that many planners go the normal progressive path through their local government. They're always sort of moving out. And so you say to them... "what would you like to do?" And they all say they want to do a Canberra and, you know, want to go down and have all these cow paddocks and build a whole new utopian city of it. And those opportunities only come along once in a hundred years. But here we've got a smaller version of it. (Thomas, interview)*

Thus the corridor was a chance for planners, perhaps more crucially than other professionals, to do something where they had control and where their expertise was relatively unchallenged. It provided a place where they could show their skills without those skills being contested by local residents, where technical planning knowledge did not need to confront local knowledge, at least too much. Particularly for those planners of the generation trained in physical planning and design, and for those influenced by Australian urbanist Hugh Stretton's championship of Canberra (Stretton 1989), Rouse Hill provided something approaching the

ideal space of a "utopian city." Not all planners saw Canberra in
this way – some saw it as merely "nice trees, grass" – but for some
it was a utopia (Alan, interview).

The Image's Shortfalls

The image of a utopian city was perhaps why plans rarely stated
in the current population of the area but focused on projections of
the future (see Peattie 1991, 36, 50). Of the published state-level
plans only the 1984 Regional Enviromental Study, covering the
broadest geographical definition of the North West Sector, at
126,000 hectares, included population figures of 82,968 in 1981
(DEP 1984a,121). In other state plans, focused more specifically
on the 9,400 hectares in the Rouse Hill Development Area, it
was treated as basically unpopulated.[8] For example, the 1991
Environmental Impact Statement for the Sewage Treatment Plant
used aerial photographs from the late 1970s in showing surround-
ing properties, highlighting only seventeen "existing residences"
in the vicinity of the proposed sewage treatment plant (Manidis
Roberts 1991, figure 14).[9] In contrast, local residents found 280
houses located in the area contained in the aerial photograph, some
new and some obscured by trees in the photograph, a "silence"
in the map (Harley 1988, 290). Further, as planners often experienced the site largely through these maps and photographs, rather
than through site visits, the silence was compounded. As one local
resident activist remarked:

> It's the land that the planners seem to look at not the
> total picture, not the environment. There's already a
> community and a lifestyle that exists in the area that's
> been totally disregarded. And when I've spoken to plan-
> ners they talked about it as remnant farmland, open
> fields, and it's really land of little importance. It's land
> that they see that can be developed and it's really the
> opposite of the way I see it. (Sarah, interview, previ-
> ously quoted)

Thus for at least one group of pro-expansion planners the corridor
was imagined as a flat field without human inhabitants, "cow paddocks" where they could develop an ideal city or at least an ideal
growth corridor. They ignored the local population, although as many

of the most vocal locals had moved in after planning had commenced, affluent enough to purchase small farms in an urbanizing area, this was perhaps a pointed omission. In any case, the corridor was the closest many would come to planning a new city and it was intensely attractive for that reason.

The image of Canberra, however, only approximated the situation in the Rouse Hill project. As a national capital, Canberra received a high level of resources in terms of funding, government good will, planning, and design. It had been placed in a rural landscape, not semi-rural one. All land in Canberra was owned by the federal government. In contrast, planning responsibilities in the Rouse Hill corridor were fragmented between state and local governments, and the private sector. The public-private Rouse Hill Infrastructure Consortium, representing the largest landowners in the area, had used state cabinet-level connections – the state Department of Housing was a member – to pressure local government planners for speedy rezonings in a generic subdivision pattern. This made sophisticated urban design difficult, although Baulkham Hills worked hard to create separate neighborhoods, Blacktown to get social services, and individual property developers to calm traffic and create entrance "statements" (e.g. Baulkham Hills Council 1993, 1994a, 1994b; Berkhout 1992). In addition, local and scientific environmentalists complained loudly to state and local planners, and to a wider public, calling for a moratorium. Given these pressures it took some work to sustain the image of the development as a benign utopia.

IMAGES AND ARGUMENTS

This growth corridor was not only a location on the edge of Sydney, it was a place in people's minds. Using the images of Los Angeles, Toronto, and Canberra, the present and the future were made simple and evocative, even if that meant screening out a host of contradictions. They were not the only metaphors or images used to describe the corridor's future, but they were powerful ones and they were also of a common kind; representing the future of one city with the name or photograph of another.

Of course in popular and academic life metaphors and images with elements of synecdoche are both ubiquitous and useful, if also partial and potentially misleading: calling a computer screen a "desktop"; a city neighborhood a university's "urban laboratory"; declaring "wars" on drugs or disease; evoking the US "wall" between church and state; seeing nations as "families," "bodies," "melting pots," or "mosaics"; describing a "backlash" against feminism.[10] Social scientists invent metaphors in creating theories; social theory is overflowing with metaphorical gatekeepers, iron cages, structures, games, and dramas.

In planning and design, metaphorical images are similarly useful, problematic, and unavoidable. Information about urban growth is frequently technical and borning and making it more accessible necessarily involves interpreting and representing it in particular ways. In many ways Los Angeles, Canberra, and Toronto were very efficient and effective images. However, choosing LA as a possible future and not Perth or Phoenix or San Francisco; choosing Canberra and not Chandigarh or Brasilia or La Defense or Milton Keynes; Toronto and not Paris or Moscow; involved a set of choices between cities that were equally as appropriate as images of sprawl or new-town planning or European-style city structure. Similarly, why choose an actual city at all when other images are possible: gridlock, oasis, machine, organism? It is a kind of choice that planners and activists frequently make as they describe a proposal as like one city and not another. It is a kind of image that may in any case be used by others to represent one's data, as the Los Angeles image was used by activists to popularize the Hyde and Johnson air quality study.

These images worked on several levels. First, while explicitly about one aspect of the cities they simultaneously evoked wider associations. Second, the images were particularly visual and seen in overview, something shaped by the strong television presence of Los Angeles and Canberra. Third, they had a regional flavor. These cities had particular meanings for people in Sydney, that would not be replicated in Cincinnati or San Diego. Fourth, the images were more representative of the overall idea that people wanted to convey than the actual details of the places, raising issues of truthfulness. Finally, they were generally empowering for professionals and activists, giving individual human agents – if relatively elite professionals and activists – a role in shaping a city, or else pointing out in a negative tone the lack or resources for this kind of role.

Like the maps and plans that planners so often dealt with, these popular images sacrificed some details for others, using figures of speech in a rich kind of shorthand. As well as metaphors, they could be read as a synecdoche where a whole is named but a part is understood; where Los Angeles represented its own smog and sprawl, and Canberra represented its planning.[11] However, in using these "semantically dense" images it was not possible to limit the images to only those aspects focused on – smog, sprawl, size, and planning (Barthes 1980; Entrekin 1991, 11, 138). Rather the synecdoche operated in the reverse direction as well, where a part is named but a whole understood, evoking a wider set of connections; not only Los Angeles but all of America or materialism or sprawl or freeways (c.f. Soja 1989); not only Canberra but all of utopian and garden-city style planning. Interestingly, in this case study, the images were generally used in one direction which was their power. For example, Los Angeles could have been used positively by environmentalists as an example of city making multi-billion dollar investments in rail and other measures for improving air quality, but this was negatively portrayed as too little and too late.

These images and metaphors tapped into broadly-held but narrowly-based understandings. Both Los Angeles and Canberra were particularly visual images, images of cities often seen in overview from aerial photographs and as background shots (c.f. Schein 1993; Peattie 1987, chapter 6). As an internationl center for the production of popular culture, Los Angeles was well known to all involved in the corridor (see also Meinig 1979, 169–172; Goring 1988). Television series like *Beverly Hills 90210* and *LA Law* were clearly located there and not just somewhere in "America," and showed a particular kind of materialistic life. Even those who had visited LA had often experienced it in a way that was focused like a video: flying in and out, driving on the freeways, looking out for the attractions they had already read about or seen on TV. Represented in Sydney's urban debates by slides of those freeways, often aerial views through the grayish haze of smog, the LA image was a kind of "still" suggesting a larger script of descent into chaos and by implication the imperative of recognizing environmental limits in Sydney. It was particularly well suited to both regional and local activist campaigns that needed to compress ideas into soundbites. In contrast, Canberra was one of the few "planned"cities in the world; green, spacious, and a little boring; a suburban utopia of modernist monuments and suburban houses. While only 300 kilometers from Sydney it was, however, likewise familiar to most Australians through video images of reporters talking in front of government buildings on the television news each night.

Los Angeles and Canberra were thus places, or perhaps more accurately landscapes,[12] that people had looked at frequently on television and could visualize in order to evaluate; they could imagine freeways and smog, trees and parliament house. However, like the images of spatially-distant locations constructed in tourist guidebooks and advertisements, these images of the temporally-distant completed growth corridor were partial and misleading (Goss 1993; Cooper 1994). This correspondence with tourist promotions is interesting but complex. Tourist material is engaged in creating a sense of the place it refers to, rather as was the case with the image of Toronto. However, the more common images of Los Angeles and Canberra relied on pre-existing understandings shaped by others and perhaps because of that evoked somecontradictory responses. A few people liked LA; others were worried about Canberra.

These verbal and visual images of the three cities were, however, powerful enough to create senses of place, even if they were to some extent imaginary and contested. In a sense, the potential of communications technologies to homogenize space had been counteracted by a new kind of regionalism the technologies had created, a regionalism of virtual landscapes located in people's minds.[13] In this virtual geography, Los Angeles and Canberra were recognizable to people in Sydney as unique places, as types (smoggy, planned), and as locations representatives of particular countries. Snapshots of the location could be retrieved from memory, cued by slides but also just by the names of these places. Although quite different to the images residents of the cities might have, these virtual images were nevertheless compelling.

This name association is also reminiscent of Hertzog et al.'s (1976) study of "preference for familiar urban places" where the researchers achieved similar results in an experimental study by using slides of local buildings, by simply listing names and locations, and by listing these names and locations followed by a brief period of mental visualization. That is "when dealing with familiar environmental settings, the use of photographs adds little not already conveyed by the place names.... [T]he reaction is not to the presented stimulus per se [such as words or image] but to a distillation of experience and knowledge of the place depicted" (Hertzog *et al.* 1976, 640–641). Although Los Angeles, Toronto, and Canberra were not part of people's local experiences but were shaped by visual media, the images gained from these media were still complex and familiar enough to enable people who heard the names to look out at the corridor and see more than smog and planning but to imagine alternate possible landscapes. Cued by the place names, and using the vocabularies, information, and experiences available to them, they could make judgments about which futures were best, while others remained unimaginable.

The interpretations were also particularly Australian takes on these images, although the general pattern of regionally shared perceptions of particular cities is likely to be a widespread phenomenon. Canberra is well known in Australia as its national captial: Australian professional planners have a high level of knowledge about Canberra's planning; the television-watching public is very familiar with pictures of its public buildings. The image of LA certainly said something about superficiality, sprawl, and materialism, but it did not seem to be linked with ideas about "crime... gangs and earthquakes" that people from the US link with Los Angeles (Till 1993, 72 Goring 1988). In the Rouse Hill debate these characteristics seemed to be linked with a more generalized image of the US or perhaps California.[14] The Los Angeles image did tap into a kind of low-level anti-American feeling within the Australian public in the early 1990s, a widespread view fed by a range of US foreign policies from wheat subsidies to defense, although perhaps not as widespread as the various environmentalists imagined. The LA image, in particular, needed heavy cueing to suppress alternative interpretations. In contrast to the Hertzog *et al.* study of individual buildings referred to above, LA is a very complex landscape and the name "Los Angeles" could have many meanings. Using pictures and accounts of smog and freeways, environmentalists suppressed the alternative positive associations with Hollywood, surf, Disneyland, economic boom, or even transit investment. By comparison, Toronto was far less well known so its image was formed in the debate itself.

This regional pattern of understandings echoes Adams'(1992) innovative discussion of television and place. Adams refers to a distinction between insider (local) and outsider (distant) television audiences where insider audiences are more likely to see programs as reflecting part of their culture, or as being fantasy, and outsider audiences are more likely to see programs as representing all of "them." As Adams points out, although this division is easy enough to make theoretically, empirical work has shown more complex patterns with, for example, some local groups perceiving themselves as outsiders. This case study confirms some of this complexity.

With a good grasp of the public's overall knowledge, and some effective cueing slides, experts such as Newman and Kenworthy and their followers tailored their talks to fit a politically cogent image, and their own overall findings, rather than the complex details of their own data. By de-emphasizing the more complex variables they oversimplified in a way that ultimately discredited them with many pro-development and pro-expansion professionals (and even pro-consolidation professionals who were concerned about issues of evidence). However, in public forums a more complex discussion may well have obscured their basic point just as the LA-Toronto image obscured their published data. This issue of simplification and (mis)representation was, and remains, a difficult issue for many researchers wishing to have public influence or to have their work taken up in public debates. It is an issue I return to below.

Even the obstensibly more benign Canberra image functioned in a similar way. The Canberra image used the corridor's size to raise resource concerns and, when addressed to other professionals, it evoked utopian city planning. This in turn enabled the current population to be imagined away, replaced by "cow paddocks" and obscuring the more complex situation of a rural residential urban fringe.

In their partiality the city images are thus reminiscent of the metaphor of the "dual" city critiqued by Marcuse (1989), where a complex set of overlapping inequalities is represented as a splitting in two, generally on the lines of income or race. This dual city image was in fact used from time to time in Sydney with the relatively well-off eastern suburbs contrasted with the disadvantaged west (e.g. Travers 1991). Marcuse explains the dual city metaphor is misleading in its ahistorical oversimplification of urban inequality. The images of Los Angeles, Toronto, and Canberra were also misleading, although through a slightly different process of simultaneously simplifying (the future as smog) and evoking wider associations (smog being inextricably mixed up with materialism, the US, and so on).

Was there, then, anything wrong in using these kinds of metaphors? Did these images mislead the public, or other professionals, in a way that was manipulative? Forester (1989, 36) has applied Habermas' criteria for unmanipulated communication to this issue of power in planning.[15] In this formulation, unmanipulated communication should be: clear and comprehensible, sincere and trustworthy, appropriate and legitimate, accurate and true. Against these criteria the Los Angeles-Toronto image would perhaps be judged as manipulation by experts. This is "perhaps" because it is not at all certain. The image was clear and can easily be seen as a sincere attempt to represent problems and possibilities for intervention. The image was arguably appropriate for people with a visionary bent talking to audiences with varied educational and professional backgrounds, and it was arguably truthful to the overall findings of various research projects if not all their details. This demonstrates a dilemma for professionals and activists addressing mixed audiences on complex matters as well as some difficulties in operationalizing Habermas' criteria for unmanipulated communication in such situations (cf. Hillier 1993).

My interest in the LA-Toronto image started because of my sense that there was something wrong with it, a sense that was confirmed by my own analyses and by others who published critiques of the work (e.g. Brindle 1992; Gordon and Richardson 1989). Some observers came to understand the LA-Toronto image as a deliberate misrepresentation of an ambiguous situation, betraying the public trust given to experts, and leaving the public ill-prepared as participants in a democratic decision-making process. I have sympathy with this position. I would not have conducted this analysis if I had found the city images to be (literally) unremarkable. The lay public and even many professionals took up the Los Angeles image, in its Newman and Kenworthy form, quite trustingly. I think it seemed so obvious to many that Los Angeles was a sprawling mess, and that Sydney must be different, that they did not even think about exploring the detailed findings. These images were not the only areas in my research where I heard and saw experts making claims that were not backed up by their own data, but they were a disturbing subset of such events. I still however see these rhetorical devices as, in general, presenting a dilemma rather than being simply dishonest.

Due to its extreme form the LA-Toronto image highlights a fundamental characteristic of metaphor, that at the base it *is* wrong in that it is claiming one thing is like another in a way that can never be totally the case. Geertz, drawing on the work of Percy (1958), argues that:

> *[Metaphor] tends to be the most effective when the most "wrong." The power of metaphor derives precisely from the interplay between the discordant meanings it symbolically coerces into a unitary conceptual framework ... . When it works, a metaphor transforms a false identification (for example of the labor policies of the Republican Party and those of the Bolsheviks) into an apt analogy; when it misfires it is mere extravagance. (Geertz 1973, 210–211)*

Of course, part of my argument is that what was disturbing about the Los Angeles, Toronto, and even Canberra, images was not only their mismatch with the situation in Sydney (the kind of wrongness Geertz is referring to), but their mismatch with the situation in Los Angeles, Toronto, and Canberra, particularly in terms of the data presented by Newman and Kenworthy. They represented these cities in sometimes partial and sometimes over-generalized ways, tapping into existing biases and creating additional ones.[16]

Interestingly, the public and private sector developers in this case did not tend to use these city images, perhaps because they had other forms of economic and institutional power that they had used very effectively to push the development along. However, this silence was in some ways specific to this case at a particular period as property developers frequently employ these kinds of place associations when naming and promoting developments.

In Rouse Hill the juxtaposed city images were useful in abbreviating quite complex arguments about causal factors in automobile use and air pollution, and urban planning, making the future of the specific corridor imaginable. Even if they inaccurately represented the present and future, they were still appealing in enabling a public to visualize that change and to see their own role in fostering or preventing that future: fighting ecological devastation, building spacious cities. The Canberra image was particularly interesting in this light: giving planners a role in creating a new city, but also warning about the probable lack of resources for that task. In providing room for individual human agency the images stand in some contrast to the disabling metaphor of "structures" of power that Marris (1987) describes in the context of Britain in the 1970s. There professionals and activists were constrained by a sense that they had to totally dismantle the structure of existing economic conditions, something that was not possible. Perhaps, however, these images were falsely enabling, like the dual city image, providing too easy a solution to a complex set of urban problems with too grand a role for professionals and activists.

These kinds of images were not, then, simple to use. They were culturally specific and even within a culture or subculture there was disagreement about their full implications. Sprawling Los Angeles was not quite such a terrifying possible future to those who liked Canberra and who knew Sydney's density was already lower. Among environmentalists it also held different meanings with those with a background in regional issues likely to fear environmental damage, those with a humanistic bent worried about socio-environmental inequalities, and those with a local focus often more offended by the LA aesthetic. Similarly, Canberra was only a utopia to a particular group of those I interviewed who were generally older and less concerned about the negative effects of suburban sprawl. The simplifications, then, raised questions about the character of design debates where complicated futures are being imagined through images that are rarely as complex.

While imperfect, these kinds of visual multi-layered city images are common and unlikely to depart. The mainstream visual media, and planning debates, will continue to portray particular places in greater and less depth, and planners, designers, and activists will be able to use their visually familiar characteristics (or the lack of them) to help a wider public imagine a particular future.[17]

In the following chapters I place the perspectives, frameworks, and images I have dealt with so far more concretely in the context of planning and debating Rouse Hill. Different groups faced each other not in some neutral landscape of ideas but in specific political contexts where the persuasive, inspirational, and identity-forming power of ideas interacted with other power relationships on an uneven and historically shifting terrain. What ideas could do was shape the character of the impacts on the urban landscape of economic, administrative, and political power.

End Notes

1   This analysis extends a subset of the work on planning communication mentioned in chapter one, work that has examined how the language of planning shapes planners' and others' imaginations in particular situations (see Mandelbaum 1990a).
2   Richmond (forthcoming) also briefly discusses this concern about Sydney becoming another Los Angeles. Recently Ewing (1997) has used the term "Los Angeles-style sprawl" in a US context but has received some criticism for this (see Gordon and Richardson 1997; Levine 1997).
3   Newman and Kenworthy considered a number of "economic factors" affecting fuel use – "the demographic size of a city, vehicle ownership, income, gasoline price and vehicle fuel efficiency" – along with a set of "social/cultural factors" – "climate related lifestyle, spatial traditions and politics" (Newman and Kenworthy 1989a, 69). However, the emphasis of their research was on the physical form of cities.
4   While Newman and Kenworthy's thesis of the contribution of land use practices to auto dependence, over and above economic factors, seems basically sound (Evill 1995), both it and their specific analyses were criticized (Brindle 1992; Gordon and Richardson 1989; Kirwan 1992; McManus 1992; Moriarty and Beed 1992). Newman and Kenworthy were, however, quite prolific in expounding their ideas about the connections between land use and transportation (see Kenworthy 1991a, 1991b; Newman 1990, 1991; Newman and Kenworthy 1989a, 1989b, 1991, 1992; also Cervero 1989, 1990; Handy 1992; Mitchell and Rapkin 1954).
5   I used Newman and Kenworthy's standardized data for these comparisons. The definition of the Los Angeles Metropolitan Area was the LA-Long Beach SMSA except in density calculations which cover a broader area. Sydney is defined as the Australian Bureau of Statistics' Sydney Statistical Division. Toronto is defined as the Municipality of Metropolitan Toronto, including only 2,137,000 of the 3,148,000 people living in the Toronto Metropolitan region (Newman and Kenworthy 1989a, 18–19).
6   Further, because Canadian vehicles had very low fuel efficiencies, per capita energy use for both public and private transport in Toronto was actually 40 percent more than the same figure in Sydney.
7   The results for the competition of Canberra's design were announced in 1912, with Burley Griffin appointed to start building in 1913 (Stretton 1989, 28).
8   Although in their background information for the Draft Local Environmental Plan, Baulkham Hills Council did note the number of existing residents in

their part of the first stage of the corridor development – 7,603 in 1986 – their discussion of the existing population was limited to one short paragraph (Baulkham Hills Shire Council 1990, table 3).

[9] The estimate of the photograph's date came from local residents, members of the group SENS.

[10] Each of these metaphors has been analyzed (see, in order, Wozny 1989; Adams 1991; McGaw 1991; Ross 1989; Stein 1990; Hammond *et al.* 1981; Morris 1984; Appadurai 1974; Stein and Hill 1977; Newson 1991).

[11] This is a figure of speech related to metonymy where words are seen to be related by "proximity be that spatial, temporal, or conceptual" (Miller 1982, 145).

[12] The word landscape originally referred to a picture of inland scenery, but over the years its meaning has been enlarged (Cosgrove 1984, 16–17). Within cultural geography *place* more commonly refers to the insiders' views of a location, *landscape* implies outsiders' views.

[13] Entrekin (1991, 28–29) contains an interesting discussion of early warnings of homogenization of place due to improved communications and transportation technologies.

[14] Writers in other parts of Australia used the LA image differently, for example referring to such characteristics as social division (e.g. Peel 1995).

[15] I should note here that Forester's work goes well beyond interpreting Habermas.

[16] Although this chapter does not attempt to undertake a full-scale semiotic analysis of the city names, these complex associations with city names relate to work in semiotics, for example that of US pragmatist Pierce. Pierce sees "signs" in three parts: "a vehicle that conveys an idea to the mind, which [Pierce] called the *representanamen*; another idea that interprets the sign, which he called the *interpretant*; and an object for which the sign stands" (Gottdiener 1995, 9). For example the word "Los Angeles" (representanamen) stands for the location called Los Angeles that exists in the world (object) but the particular meaning Los Angeles takes on depends on the idea (the interpretant) that exists in people's minds about these objects. As this chapter has described there was some disagreement about the meaning of these city names, with dominant views resisted by minorities.

To Lyotard, and others more critical of any claims to transparent truths, discussing manipulation may itself be misleading as what is occurring is a kind of clash of language games with different rules (Lyotard 1984, 65–66). The LA-Toronto image in this sense can be seen as part of a political language game and to judge it as detailed technical description is to unfairly impose on it a different set of rules.

[17] That these images are likely to oversimplify and misrepresent is a cause for concern. This research cannot, however, come up with a neat condemnation of their use.

CHAPTER FOUR

Formal Planning Processes: The Privileged Language of Professional Planning

Although Rouse Hill is a place to the north west of currently urbanized Sydney, the Rouse Hill Development Area was the creation of a formal planning process that has already spread across three decades. By transforming a group of farms, houses, and small-scale work places into a 'Sector' and then a 'Development Area', the formal planning processes focused attention away from the existing landscape and toward the changes that would occur in the area. It set the agenda both conceptually in terms of the shape of the development as a growth corridor, and literally in terms of the many formal meetings that occurred during the long planning process. Of course not everyone has to follow an agenda, particularly when it is set by someone else far in advance of the actual development and in a context of fairly rapid change. In Rouse Hill the agenda was increasingly questioned. These questions transformed suburban development from a social good into an environmental and economic problem, at least for some participants.

This chapter gives an account of Rouse Hill's formal planning as it faced changes in infrastructure finance and housing affordability along with rising citizen and bureaucratic awareness about air and water quality issues. These components – plans, finance, affordability, pollution – were the things that planners, property developers, environmental and human service bureaucrats, residents, and activists talked about and fought over. They were the issues that slowed the project and reshaped its direction into the 1990s.

First, I explain some of the context of the formal planning process in Rouse Hill along with its bureaucratic politics. For many people, particularly those in government, this was the most basic

story of the Rouse Hill Development Area. Without this formal
planning process few changes would have occurred in the area and
those that did occur would likely have been more gradual. I then
explore the process of citizen participation and of the representation
of public needs; describe debates over infrastructure financing and
priorities; trace the history of increasing awareness of water pollution; and introduce the range of publicly debated alternatives to
Sydney's urban expansion, from stopping immigration to reshaping
urban form. As problems emerged a series of adjustments and com-
promises enabled Rouse Hill to continue, although the original goal
of providing detached houses for first-home buyers was increasingly
undermined. Throughout the project's history, state and local planners tried to use the formal planning process to gain some control
over other participants in the development process, but they were
only partly successful.

Formal Planning

As I explained in chapter one, although the 1968 Sydney Region
Outline Plan projected that the main development of the North West
Sector Would start in 1980, Sydney's slower than anticipated population growth meant that it was not until 1981 that even preliminary
planning commenced (SPA 1968, 95; DEP 1982, 36). Beginning in
1984, a series of publicly available environmental studies and plans
– broad land use planning exercises carried out by the New South
Wales state planning agency – were produced. These were followed
by more detailed local plans, the zoning and urban design instruments, carried out by the two local councils (see chronology and
figure 7). Literally dozens of plans, studies, impact statements, and
determinations were produced by state and local governments, and
consultants, in the decade leading up to the start of construction.
Many were part of the legally defined planning sequence of Regional Environmental Study, Regional Environmental Plan, Local
Environmental Plan, and Development Control Plan.
    Although in hindsight this process seems quite formal and pre-
dictable, following a pattern laid out in legislation, the exact scope
and timing of each study and plan was actually open to quite a
wide range of discretion. Under the Environmental Planning and
Assessment Act, the Director of the Department of Planning was

1968	Sydney Regional Outline Plan: North West Sector indicated for future investigation for urban development.
1980	December: Development Coordinating Committee of state cabinet requests structure plan for North West Sector .
1982	January: Structure Plan presented to Urban Development Committee.
1984	July: North West Sector Regional Environmental Study released for public comment.
1986	October: Rouse Hill Development Area North West Sector Draft Regional Environmental Plan released.
1988	New metropolitan plan published.
1989	September: Rouse Hill Development Area Regional Environmental Plan made official.
1990	June: Draft Local Environmental Plans for Parklea Release Area, (Blacktown City Council) and Kellyville-Rouse Hill (Baulkham Hills Shire Council) released.
1991	Environmental Impact Statement for proposed sewage treatment plant released.
1991	Local Environmental Plans for Parklea and Kellyville/Rouse Hill Release Areas gazetted.
1991	June: Determining Authority's Report (acceptance) of Environmental Impact Statement for sewage treatment plant.
1993-1994	Development Control Plans for Parklea and Kellyville/Rouse Hill.
1995	New metropolitan plan published.

Figure 7 Formal Planning Process Summary

given the ability to prepare a draft Regional Environmental plan for the region or issue that was "in the opinion of the Director, of significance for environmental planning for the region"(NSW 1979, section 40). Section 51 gave the Minister the ability to include "such matters as are, in his opinion, of significance for environmental planning for the region." Section 52 gave the Minister the authority to determine "the regulations, the format, structure and subject matters" of a Regional Environmental Plan or draft Regional Environmental Plan. Generally this led to two types of plans – some dealing with broad strategy in a region, and others rezoning an area of regional significance – but the room for latitude was significant (DEP 1984a,

253–254). Similar variations existed in the scope and content of Regional Environmental Studies, Local Environmental Plans, and Development Control Plans with the Director of Planning or the Minister given broad powers (see NSW 1979, sections 41, 57).

This flexibility in interpretation was the subject of some conflict throughout the planning process as different government departments and authorities tried to gain control over the development agenda. For example, an alteration to the minutes of the August 1983 meeting of the interdepartmental Urban Development Committee indicated that the decision to undertake the Regional Environmental Study was taken by the planning agency "without prior consultation with either the Sub-committee set up to advise on the development of the NW Sector or the relevant Ministers" (Urban Development Committee 12 December 1983). Putting Rouse Hill on the "statutory" planning track of Regional Environmental Study and Regional Environmental Plan in the early 1980s was seen by many "as a political step by the Department of Planning so they wouldn't lose control of the planning process to the Department of Housing who own[ed] substantial amounts of land in the area" (Eric, interview).

However, far from providing detailed specifications about the development's form, the Regional Environmental Study and Regional Environmental Plan were very general in content. This is particularly obvious in the graphical representation of the REP where most of the area was undifferentiated except for some industrial areas, flooding zones, and the regional center. This was a rather vague concept diagram for an area planned to house a quarter of a million people. Those I interviewed at the local government level commented on this negatively (see figure 8).

While this process formally enabled the Department of Planning to coordinate other departments, it turned out to be a week coordination mechanism. Canberra, a city of a similar size to the proposed Rouse Hill Development Area, had been planned by a semi-autonomous development body, the National Capital Development Commission, that had proved far more powerful. The Macarthur Growth Area around Campbelltown in the South West Sector had also been developed under a separate Development Corporation, originally within the Department of Environment and Planning (Meyer 1990, 25). However, Rouse Hill did not use these mechanisms.

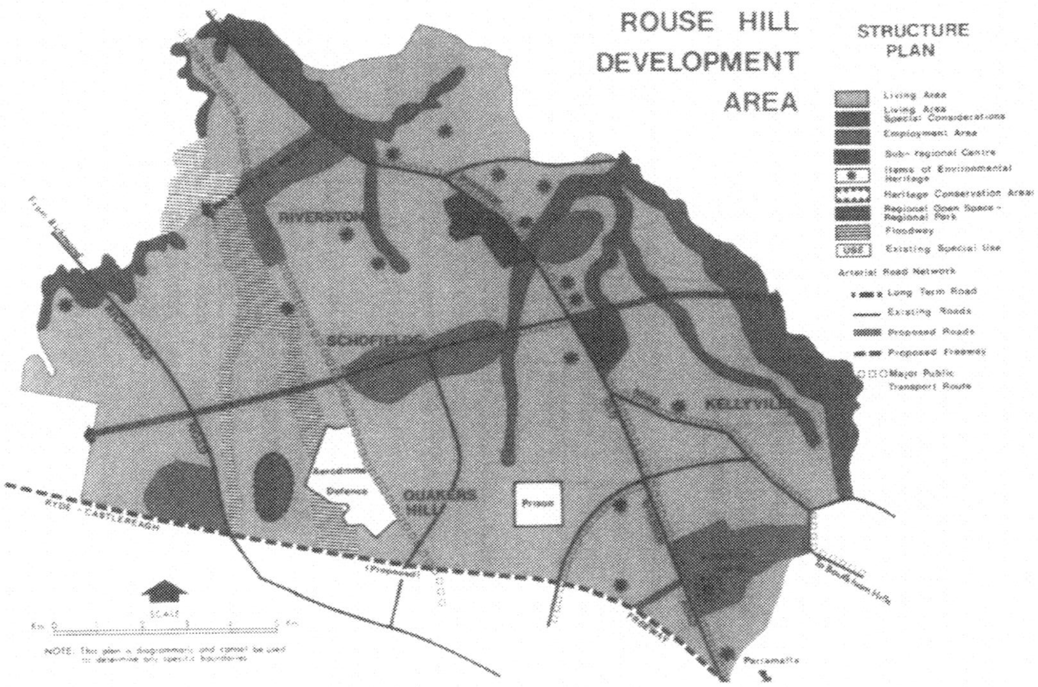

Figure 8 Regional Environmental Plan Graphic

Reproduced from **Rouse Hill Development Area**, Sydney Regional Environmental Plan Number 19 (1989) with permission from the NSW Department of Urban Affairs and Planning, Australia.

Public Participation

While the slow planning process seemed to allow generous time
of public comment, various government agencies actually held tight
control. In the early 1980s, attempts were made to limit public
access to plans because they provided a "speculators guide" (Frank,
interview).[1] Once the public planning process started, direct participation by members of the public was generally confined to reacting to plans, often at short notice, rather than participating in
their drafting. This occurred equally for local and regional planning. Finally, in the early 1990s, public participation and access to
information was further limited through privatization. Throughout
the process information was provided either in excess – mountains
of detail to be slowly waded through – or in schematic form with
many details missing.

Further, as one local environmentalist pointed out, public submissions were required at each stage of the multi-step formal planning process.[2] Rather than a collaboration or a conversation, the
process became a "war of attrition" (Sarah, interview). People had
to keep objecting to keep their concerns under consideration but
could only do so when the planning process allowed it. As far as I
can tell, the only public meetings called by government authorities, at least until the middle of 1992, were Blacktown's oral submission section of their Local Environmental Plan Environmental
Impact Statement.

During the 1980s and 1990s, a small number of public meetings
were, however, called by community groups. The Western Sydney
Action Group held meetings in Richmond and Blacktown in March
and July 1985 and produced a short-lived newsletter *People Building Community: A Community Response to Proposed Developments
in Sydney's North West*. Six years later, in November 1991, another
public meeting was held attracting 120 people. The speakers included members of parliament and local environmental activists,
and passed the unanimous motion: "that this meeting expresses its
total opposition to further urban development in [the] North West
Sector until complete guarantees are provided of all and adequate
infrastructure and environmental measures to the satifaction of the
community of the area" (Minutes of the... 1991,5; Hills Mercury
1991). The Rouse Hill Community Planning Team, a coalition of

human service providers, held a public meeting about social service issues in October 1992 and held another with existing community groups 1993 (see chapter five).

Of course, direct participation of citizens in a planning process – whether in reaction to plans or through some more robust mechanism – is only one way of having people's ideas and interests represented in the planning process. In interviews some planners were cynical about the whole idea of existing residents participating in planning for release areas.

> *Who you really ought to be talking to [are] the fifty thousand people who are going to come and live in there. And they don't know they're going to come and live in there and all the people, the only people that make a submission are the ones who basically see that your plan is affecting their chance of making millions in a couple of years. And they want you to change that, often not in the best way for the ultimate community. (Eric, interview)*

In Rouse Hill, planners and activists were adept at representing the needs of the various publics they related to without having to hold public meetings. They did this though such mechanisms as social statistics, professional observations, and measurements of effects on the natural world.

In new areas, public participation also faces dilemmas about private speculation, particularly in situations without massive government land holdings. Early in the planning process there were such proposals for significant government land ownership. The Development Area became, however, a largely private sector development with public sector guidance (DEP 1984b, 21). This private sector role was extended in the late 1980s when the Department of Housing, as part of a consortium with private developers, proposed privately financing water services (see chapter five).

A final issue to do with public input was a sluggishness in using new data. I, like many of the activists I interviewed, was quite surprised at how repetitious the plans were. A number of consultant studies, as well as reports by other government departments, were prepared throughout out process.[3] Once collected, however, data for the early reports were used and reused in later reports even though the slow planning process meant that conditions had changed. More importantly perhaps, data not collected in the early 1980s were not collected later either. As local activist complained:

> *I think that part of the problem with this North West Sector development is a lot of the initial decisions were made with the wrong information at hand. They didn't know about the storm water problem. They didn't know about the traffic problem. When these original decisions were made to go ahead with this [development], these very vital pieces of information weren't looked at. And because they weren't looked at they've just continually been overlooked and ... it's just going to mean devastation for the whole region of Sydney, because the wrong premises have been used to start. (Sarah, interview)*

Reusing data certainly gave reports consistency and saved planning time. This may well have been appropriate under more stable conditions. In Rouse Hill, however, it locked in assumptions that could be criticized as outdated.

Infrastructure Costs and Financing

In Australia, housing has long been a major policy issue. Australians expect governments to intervene in the housing market in order to promote home ownership and, at least sometimes, public housing. Detached housing has remained popular in Australia and government support for fringe suburban development has allowed both low-income families and more affluent groups to buy into this housing form, or to at least rent it. A number of studies conducted in Sydney have documented this support. Thorne *et al.* (1980), in an interview survey, found 90 percent of the 990 respondents preferred detached housing over other types, although in 1986 only 68 percent of Sydney's dwellings were free-standing houses (Thorne 1983, 1991).

In Sydney the state government had, over the years, directly provided rental public housing, funded community (non-profit) housing, sold public housing, acted as a land banker and land developer, and provided a wide range of infrastructure. By the late 1980s, however, the practice of governments financing fringe suburban expansion had come under question due to three major changes: increases in real interest rates, government aversion to increased deficits, and the rising cost of infrastructure provision on the fringe.

In the late 1970s and early 1980s federal policies deregulated the Australian financial system. This led to an increase in foreign debt mainly due to private corporate borrowing. From 1945 to 1980, a period of major urban growth and thus of borrowing for urban infrastructure, real interest rates had averaged around one percent per year. The period of deregulation either caused or coincided with, depending on one's interpretation, an increase in real interest rates that reached 8 percent in 1989 before falling. This increase severely reduced the amount of debt borrowers, including governments, could service (Gregory 1991; Kirwan 1991, 4).[4]

At the same time the federal government reduced the amount governments (including state and local levels) could borrow. The New South Wales "global borrowing limit" for both state and local governments dropped from AUS$ 1,940 million in the 1984–1985 financial year, and $2,060 million in 1985–1986, to $1,144 million in 1989–1990 (NSW 1992a, 2). While it was unclear whether these figures were in constant or current dollars, in either case the reduction in borrowing was quite dramatic.

Meanwhile the costs of providing physical infrastructure on the fringe of Sydney increased. The remaining undeveloped sites in the region were physically difficult to service and over time environmental standards became more stringent. Rouse Hill, in particular, had few existing services to build on. As one development professional explained:

> People find it difficult to visualize that we're talking about an area of something like five and a half thousand hectares [in the first stage], and there are [new] services [needed] all over that area. It's probably, I think somebody said to me it's the biggest urban release area in Sydney's history and I think it's probably close ... [and] there have been a lot of problems that people just didn't anticipate in the first place, and that's tended to delay it past where the private sector would have liked it. (Timothy, interview)

A major shift in the practice of fringe development was being tested at Rouse Hill.

The 1988 Metropolitan Strategy had projected that the population of the outer suburban areas would rise from 60 percent of the metropolitan figure in 1986 to 70 percent in 2011. For the Strategy's target population of 4.5 million people, 323,000 to 358,000 of the 588,000 new dwellings would be on the fringe and aimed at "low income families who are purchasing their first homes" (DoP 1988, 11). Although grounded in the expansionist ethic of providing fringe suburban housing for first-home buyers, the Metropolitan Strategy began to raise the issue of increasing infrastructure costs across the region.

> *Detached houses are popular and on the urban fringe such dwellings tend to be less expensive than detached houses elsewhere in the Region. However, the whole community pays dearly for continued urban expansion. The costs of providing physical and community services for new urban areas have to be met by Local and State Governments. Only a fraction of these costs is recoverable from developers and home buyers. In new growth sectors it is estimated that Government will bear a net cost of $20,000 ($1987) per lot for services ranging from water and sewerage to community and education facilities. (DoP 1988, 11)*

As the Metropolitan Strategy warned, these "implied subsidies" were likely to "increase substantially" (DoP 1988, 11). Combined with the locational disadvantage experienced by low-income fringe dwellers, these increasing infrastructure costs began to make providing cheap infrastructure for fringe expansion seem a misguided approach to increasing housing quality for low-income people. Moreover, in the year that the Metropolitan Strategy was published the cost of the same package of physical and social services in the Rouse Hill area was estimated at $53,300 (see table 2). This figure did not include the developer costs of $21,100 per lot for local roads, water, electricity, and fees. The estimate of the unrecouped cost to government in 1988 dollars was $30,000 per lot. In 1991 a report in the *Telegraph Mirror* put the cost of servicing a residential block at Rouse Hill at $71,525 compared with $50,000 average for the nation (Farr 1991, 8). The report did not indicate exactly which services were included. As journalist Carmel Travers (1991) declared on a television special *City Limits*: " The question must be asked; can we really afford Rouse Hill?"

TABLE 2
ROUSE HILL INFRASTRUCTURE COST ESTIMATES

	Costs per Lot Rouse Hill ($1988)	Developer Contributions ($1988)
Physical Services		
Water, sewerage, drainage	9,000	9,000
Main roads	14,900	2,200
Public transport	2,000	
Local government	7,300	7,300
Electricity	800	800
Gas	2,000	2,000
Telecom [phone]	2,000	2,000
Total	38,000	23,300
Social Services		
Police, pre-college education, family and community services, health		
Total	15,300	
Total Infrastructure by Government		
(physical and social)	53,300	
Direct Developer Costs		
Local subdivision roads and drainage	13,000	
Sewerage	1,700	
Water reticulation	1,300	
Electricity	1,500	
Landscaping	500	
Council fees	100	
Professional fees	2,000	
Total	20,100	
Broadacre land costs	30,000	
Developer's cost	73,400	
Price to home purchaser	100,000+	

Source: *NSW (1992b, 19)*.

This recognition of the high cost of infrastructure provision in new areas reinforced a long-term trend toward the government increasing the amount of infrastructure costs that it collected at the time of development. This trend applied to a variety of infrastructure components. In existing areas where most services were already available private sector developers were charged for all additional services, but on the fringe where most services had to be specially laid the practice into the 1980s was to charge property developers only about 60 percent of the cost (Hughes Trueman Ludlow 1991, x; NHS 1991d, 66). The move was to make this percentage higher.

The effects of these changing practices of infrastructure finance were the cause of some debate in professional circles, particularly relating to issues of equity or fairness, and efficiency.[5] In the early 1990s the federal government's Industry Commission conducted an "Inquiry into Taxation and Financial Policy Impacts on Urban Settlements" and the Federal Parliament's Standing Committee for Long Term Strategies examined urban settlement patterns.

Several common understandings emerged along with some severe conflicts. In terms of areas of agreement, local roads and connections to various utilities on, or close to, individual lots were generally seen as the responsibility of property developers. For the remaining infrastructure people generally separated physical infrastructure such as main roads, water, and electricity from recurrent human services funding. Parks and the buildings housing human services occupied an ambiguous intermediate space.

In equity terms most groups agreed that recurrent funding for human services should come from general taxation – collected nationally but usually distributed through the state – as it was tied to population rather than location. There was quite a bit of disagreement, however, over paying for physical and intermediate infrastructure. Some argued the move to have home buyers pay for infrastructure up front was shutting lower-income and working-class first-home buyers out of the fringe suburban market. Others pointed out that this was no longer the group moving to the fringe, but a higher income group were "trading up" to extremely large homes. This group should pay the full cost. In support of this contention they pointed out that the size of new houses had increased from 130 square meters to 180 square meters between the early 1970s and the early 1990s (NHS 1991a, 38). There were many more sticky questions, however, about physical infrastructure; should regional dams and local pipes be paid for in the same way? Integrating physical and social infrastructure was difficult; for example, local governments were allowed to collect contributions for constructing child care centers but could not be sure the state would pay to staff them.

Whatever the specific details, Rouse Hill was being developed in an era of a new kind of suburban development. As one planner remarked: "The big difference is, and it's yet to be shown, is that the outer areas are not for low-income people anymore. It has completely changed that around" (Frank, interview).

Water Quality

The Department of Housing and private developer consortium proposal for funding water works not only responded to changes in government policy and in infrastructure finance but coincided with a period of changing perceptions about water pollution issues. For all of the eastern part of Sydney, and much of the currently urbanized west, sewage flows to oceanside treatment plants that discharge effluent into the sea. Sewage treatment in Sydney was controversial in the late 1980s as few of the oceanside treatment plants treated sewage even to full primary level and beach pollution was a growing problem. The Water Board's first solution was an extension of the ocean outfalls and a public relations campaign (Beder 1989, 110). Continuing problems resulted in a revised plan to treat effluent to at least secondary level with options for upgrading this later (Water Board 1991a).

However, only a very small part of the southern edge of the Rouse Hill Development Area drained into the ocean outfall system. Sewage effluent from the vast majority of the area would flow into the Hawkesbury-Nepean River, a situation that in the 1990s became almost as controversial as the ocean outfalls.

For Rouse Hill, the 1982 "Structure Plan" had set out the options that guided development for the next decade; that a very high level of treatment must be provided or else other uses of the river would essentially have to be abandoned.

> *Distance from the coast makes the N.W. Sector unsuitable for an ocean outfall system of sewerage and*

urban run-off would be discharged into the Hawkes-
bury-Nepean River system. This could only be achieved
at the expense of other competing uses associated with
the River; namely recreation and irrigation. The
Hawkesbury is considered to be nearing maximum pol-
lutant carrying capacity and the River has only lim-
ited reserves to satisfactorily accommodate sewerage
discharge. Therefore the M.W.S. & D. [Water] Board
and the State Pollution Control Commission require
nutrient removal before any effluent can be discharged
into the Hawkesbury River system. (DEP 1982, 18)

The 1984 Regional Environmental Study again noted the problems that urban runoff and increased sewage effluent flows would cause the river. The main problem was eutrophication, "the nutrient enrichment (or over-fertilization) of waterways which may cause changes to the characteristics of the water and the aquatic life it supports" (DEP 1984a, 89). It referred to State Pollution Control Commission (SPCC) recommendations for technical solutions to these problems: providing stormwater drainage detention basins to "prevent first flush pollution loads entering natural watercourses," reducing nutrients in effluent, and reusing effluent through means such as irrigation (DEP 1984a, 87–89, 93; SPCC and Water Board 1985).

By the late 1980s, however, the water quality problems, or at least the perception of those problems, had increased in severity.[6] Even the 1988 Metropolitan Strategy, otherwise quite optimistic about pollution trends, recommended against further development in areas "where environmental impacts are likely to present special problems and it is practicable to avoid urban development .... Areas draining into the Hawkesbury Nepean River system clearly fall within this category" (DoP 1988, 27).

As a representative of the Water Board pointed out:

One of the reasons that people enjoy living in western
Sydney is the amenity that the river offers – the para-
dox is that unless controlled, there is a risk that each
successive development will lead to further deteriora-
tion in water quality. The worst case scenario is that
continual urban expansion will ultimately result in a

biologically dead river which no one wishes to live near.
While this is some time away, it is brought much closer
every time a development decision is made in isolation
from other legitimate existing or proposed uses in the
catchment and without regard to cumulative impacts
and long term sustainability. (Dodds 1991, n.p.)

Before the Rouse Hill development the catchment already contained 23 sewage treatment plants for 480,000 people and supplied the vast majority of Sydney's water. The Hawkesbury-Nepean catchment also involved a complex set of administrative arrangements: 12 State Ministerial Portfolios, approximately 20 major government agencies, over 20 local government agencies, approximately 30 state and federal members of parliament, and the Nepean-Hawkesbury Catchment Management Council (NHCMC) (Dodds 1991, n.p.). Also interested in the river were a set of private parties: industries reliant on the river for fishing, sand extraction, and tourism; environmental groups; recreational users; and nearby residents.

While initial design work on the Rouse Hill treatment plant had occurred in the early 1980s before much heated debate about water quality, the public environmental impact assessment process occurred in the late 1980s with the consortium proposal (Camp Scott Furphy 1984; Water Board 1985). Problems with water quality attracted public attention, so the river became an increasingly important part of the planning agenda. As one senior planner explained: "The Department of Planning just follows trends. Now all of a sudden there is a lot about it in the newspapers so it's going to respond to it" (Claude, interview). By the time of detailed planning for the Rouse Hill sewage treatment plant, a significant group of decision makers had realized that water quality in the Hawkesbury-Nepean River might not be amenable to technical solutions.

Before that time I think the Water Board had thought
that the treatment plant was going to, if you put in the
world's most sophisticated treatment plant then you'd
have no water quality problems. But by late 1989... I
became aware that the EIS for the [Rouse Hill] treat-
ment plant that was being done was showing that there
may be adverse impacts that couldn't be managed un-
less very innovative sorts of things could be done.
(Helen, interview)

Planned for construction in six stages, each serving 50,000 people, the sewage treatment plant was both controversial in itself, as well as the major infrastructure component required for the whole development to occur (Water Board 1991b, 5). As such it had far wider implications that mere waste water treatment and became a focus for opposition to Rouse Hill. In its determination, or evaluation, of the Rouse Hill Environmental Impact Statement document, the Water Board made this explicit.

> *Of course the implications of such a major component of the physical infrastructure of the North West Sector, and one of the first components to be constructed, are much wider than the sewage treatment plant and its direct impacts. In one sense the whole of the urban development in the North West Sector hangs on the proposal. (Water Board 1991b, 7)*

The Water Board went on to highlight the tensions it faced in its judgments, given what at least some at the Board now saw as questionable assumptions of the regional planning process.

> *There must be some presumption that planning for the North West Sector considered the macro-environmental impacts, including regional water resources impacts, such that environmental determinations for essential component infrastructure would focus on local impacts. Unfortunately, this is not a reasonable presumption in this case with the regional planning for the area being underlined by the presumption that technical solutions will be able to correct adverse environmental impacts. (Water Board 1991b, 7)*

Given the context of the earlier Water Board and metropolitan planning decisions, however, the plant had to be designed within the framework of technical solutions. As outlined in the Environmental Impact Statement, the plant included an array of post-tertiary treatments such as artificial wetlands (to absorb nutrients) and rapids (to increase oxygen), and a second set of pipes allowed use of treated sewage effluent for toilet flushing and irrigation (Manidis Roberts 1991). Many of these measures were unique in Australia and all added to the capital cost of the development. Even combined with concerns over air quality dealt with in the previous chapter, however, these problems with water infrastructure were not enough to stop Rouse Hill totally.

Alternatives to Growth

Given these concerns over costs and pollution a number of alternatives to fringe growth were suggested. Three stood out: stopping population growth, consolidating existing areas, and decentralizing urban development out of the Sydney region. By the 1980s, the last was considered by politicians and planners in Sydney as too expensive so population policies and consolidation formed the focus of the debate. By the time of the 1995 metropolitan plan, however, refocusing some growth to nearby Wollongong and Newcastle was proposed as a kind of compromise decentralization (DoP 1995; c.f. Development Corporation of New South Wales 1969).

Throughout the postwar era Sydney's population growth proved to be relatively unpredictable as it was linked to the volatile national immigration program. As I explained in chapter one, the 1980s was a period of high immigration. The peak growth through immigration occurred in 1989. If immigration was what was driving Sydney's growth many in the early 1990s, before the subsequent immigration drop became evident, believed that preventing immigration would eliminate the need for Rouse Hill.

The environmental, social, and infrastructure impacts of immigration had been a focus of debate in Australia for some time. The "Blainey Debate" of 1984 was one of the most famous contributions. It was initiated by a prominent historian who questioned the Australian public's ability to adjust to high levels of Asian immigration. The subsequent controversy culminated in a federal inquiry that supported continuing a non-racial immigration policy with a high number of immigrants (Collins 1988; Committee to Advise on Australia's Immigration Policies 1988).[7]

In the context of this recent history it was easy to accuse environmentalists advocating cuts in immigration of being anti-Asian, or at least unrealistic about the foreign policy implications of reducing the intake. Many environmentalists were vulnerable to these criticisms. It was, however, not clear whether stopping immigration would actually stop population growth in Sydney. At times of high immigration from overseas there was also high out-migration of long-term Sydney residents keeping overall growth fairly stable (Vipond and Ho 1992).[8] Further, as immigration was a national policy, the state government, and those hoping to shape its policy, turned to acting where they could, in the policy of controlling the growth of developed urban land through urban consolidation.

Urban consolidation was first used as a term to indicate building additional dwellings within the urbanized area. Its definition was later expanded to include developing fringe areas at increased densities (DoP 1991d). Under the first definition of urban consolidation, population growth did not necessarily lead to growth at the fringe. Under the second definition it was assumed to occur in a part of the fringe, unlike Rouse Hill, with good access and easy servicing. The consolidation emphasis was theoretically on increasing densities around existing services and transport, although sometimes its implementation fell short of this ideal. The policy was supported by a variety of rationales including reducing infrastructure costs, locational disadvantage, and environmental damage, as well as increasing housing choice.

Consolidation was not a new policy and throughout its history it had been controversial. Following the 1948 Cumberland Plan, the Housing Commission and private developers aligned in a pro-expansion push to undermine the plan's vision of a compact city.

> In studies published by the [Cumberland County C]ouncil on the Economics of Urban Expansion (1958) it was clear that council saw considerable virtue in firmly consolidating growth within the existing urban areas bounded by the Green Belt. But by 1959 pressure by the Housing Commission, from developers who had acquired tracts of Green Belt land in the expectation of retraction of its boundaries, and the local councils had become too strong to resist. (Harrison 1971, 125)

In this context, the 1967 prelude document to the Sydney Region Outline Plan virtually wrote off consolidation as a practical alternative, particularly given that increases in inner area dwelling numbers were also counteracted strongly by declining household sizes.

> It should be noted that although the number of dwellings in the City of Sydney and the Eastern and Inner-Sub-

*urbs increased by 14,000 between 1947–66, the popu-
lation of these areas declined by about 80,000 over the
same period. This has to be taken into account in arguments sometimes advanced that Sydney's population
growth should be accommodated by redevelopment in
the inner areas instead of by additions on the periph-
ery. (SPA 1967, 17, cf. 31; also SPA 1968, 9)*

In 1982, a Draft Medium Density Housing Policy was withdrawn
following 13,000 written submissions (Munro-Clark and Thorne
1987, 27).

The 1988 Metropolitan Strategy, although cataloguing the "continued decline in population of the inner and middle suburbs" was,
however, more hopeful about accommodating growth in existing
areas (DoP 1988, 9).

*The distribution of population within the Sydney Re-
gion is largely determined by the location of new housing. The distribution of housing in turn tends to be
dependent on the location of available land and the
level of government support for development in specific areas. The extent that additional housing is
provided in the built-up areas compared to the level of
growth in the new areas will depend on these contingencies. (DoP 1988, 9)*

In the early 1990s, the state Minister of Planning started to promote minimum fringe densities of 15 lots per gross hectare, up
from yields of 8 in the early 1980s, and the federal government
talked about national density targets (Webster 1991, n.p.; DHHCS
1992a, 12). A state policy released in 1991 enabled the Minister of
Planning to over-ride local councils to rezone vacant sites for multi-
unit housing (see DoP 1991d, 1991e). Local governments in outer
areas, faced with growth pressures, also supported consolidation
even in their own municipalities.

The state liberal government was, however, internally split on
the issue and these internal clashes were quite public by the early
1990s "with the Minister for Housing, Mr. Schipp, vigorously
promoting mostly older-style [low-density] housing developments
on the city's fringes while the Minister for Planning, Mr. Webster,
favored higher density housing" (Cook 1991b, 6). The manager

of the Water Board was quoted as a "strong supporter of urban consolidation" (Moore 1991, 3; Wilson 1990). The 1995 metropolitan plan was largely on the side of consolidation.

Each alternative – consolidation or fringe expansion – meant large losses to some group. Property developers with fringe urban land, including the Department of Housing, risked losing a huge investment if their land remained undeveloped, while other government agencies were faced with huge capital costs if expansion occurred. Although infrastructure costs might be lower in consolidation, some construction costs were higher due to union classifications (that sharply divided houses on individual lots from other construction), more stringent government regulations, and high land prices in areas attractive enough for location to be traded off against size (Bird 1991b, n.p.; Roseth 1992). Union workers, government regulators, and land owners in existing areas would gain from the process of consolidation, and builders and non-union subcontractors would lose. While many argued that continued unchanneled urban growth would lead to declining air and water quality, a matter of great concern to existing residents and environmentalists, consolidation also had negative effects in reducing the options for home buyers to obtain new detached houses, an option regarded as an inalienable right by a significant proportion of Australians (Woolcott Research 1990, 40–43; Leyshon 1992).

In this controversial situation, attempts were made to quantify the advantages and disadvantages of different growth patterns.[9] Although calculating the full cost of infrastructure was a difficult task, several studies were carried out in Australian capital cities in the late 1980s finding significant cost savings on local physical infrastructure through consolidation (e.g. Neilson Associates 1987). In Sydney a Department of Planning study of four areas, including Rouse Hill, had found these savings occurred under a variety of fringe lot size and consolidation density scenarios, even where augmentation or replacement of physical services such as sewers was necessary (Hughes Trueman Ludlow 1991).[10]

According to the Hughes Trueman Ludlow and Dwyer Leslie study of the *Public Sector Cost Savings of Urban Consolidation*, cost savings to state local governments ranged from $7,857 to $14,075 per dwelling at 1989–1990 prices. Overall savings to the community varied from $17,038 to $30,684 per dwelling. Government costs included sewerage, water, stormwater, gas, power, and telephone. Community costs added local roads and some other charges. The costings excluded public transport and main roads (Hughes Trueman Ludlow 1991, ii–v). I expect that adding public transport and main roads would only reinforce the findings of significant savings.

Groups such as the Housing Industry Association questioned the assumptions behind these cost benefit analyses.

> *Part of the response to the recognition of the supply side problems in the housing industry has been to argue that urban consolidation strategies must be developed and implemented. As essential as such strategies may be to meeting increased housing demand in already large sprawling cities, it is not clear that they will achieve as large economies in associated infrastructure investment as is often assumed. The pressures on existing infrastructure – including roads and public transport, water, sewerage and drainage systems and social and community facilities – may well bring forward necessary expenditures on refurbishment and augmentation. There may be excess capacity in some infrastructure services (e.g.sewerage) but not necessarily in others (e.g.roads and public transport). (HIA 1990,69–70; see also HIA 1992)*

This was further complicated by difficulties assessing the costs and benefits to different parts of the community of regional facilities such as opera houses and cricket grounds disproportionately located at the center of Sydney. Although this placement was largely for historical reasons, and had the advantage of superior public transport access, it still gave an infrastructure advantage to the center. Others pointed out that as residential uses made up only part of the urban area, increasing residential densities would have only a limited effect on sprawl.

The arguments of groups like the Housing Industry Association, were in turn questioned in terms of specific infrastructure components by groups like the Water Board:

> *As some of the Board's infrastructure in the older suburbs is ageing and in need of repair or replacement,*

> *expenditure on these systems will be necessary irrespec-*
> *tive of consolidation taking place. Urban consolida-*
> *tion will help to maintain the populations in areas where*
> *it has been declining, thus utilising existing systems*
> *more efficiently and making the replacement of ageing*
> *infrastructure more cost-effective. (Water Board 1991c,*
> *4–5)*

The Water Board was also in the process of identifying areas where declining household sizes had led to excess capacity.

A larger issue, beyond the potential for cost savings, involved the equity implications of changing urban form, and the way services were priced and paid for, two separate issues that were often linked in the consolidation debate. This passage from Westerman's report to WSROC outlines the dilemma.

> *The proposition of charging the full costs [of physical*
> *infrastructure] in new urbanising areas raises an im-*
> *portant equity issue which needs to be addressed. Ex-*
> *isting urban areas of Sydney have been developed with*
> *hidden subsidies and without the higher environmental*
> *standards which are demanded today and [these*
> *developments] have contributed to the water and air*
> *pollution which now force a radical change in devel-*
> *opment practices. These areas enjoy a high level of ac-*
> *cessibility and services, which is not reflected in rates*
> *and charges. Why should the new areas be required to*
> *bear the full infrastructure cost when those in existing*
> *areas do not? (Westerman 1991, n.p.)*

The Water Board proposed an alternative view.

> *The concept of equity is often taken to mean continued*
> *promotion of the quarter acre block (because that's what*
> *everyone else has) and no up front infrastructure pay-*
> *ments (because it wasn't done before) and is somewhat*
> *nefarious. If we are interested in having sustainable hous-*
> *ing development and sustainable environments, etc., then*
> *the mistakes and excessive resource consumption of the*
> *past cannot be continued under the guise of equity, just*
> *as environmental rigour is demand to a greater extent*
> *now than in the past. (Water Board 1991c, 8–9)*

Unresolved, these issues of equity, financing, sustainability, and the roles of suburban housing in the Australian way of life, were crucial background to debates over Rouse Hill as consolidation was the major alternative to its development (see also Murphy and Burnley 1990, 173–174).

Planning and Change

The years from 1968 were years of change in the planning context of Rouse Hill, as they were for many places. In particular the period of the late 1980s and early 1990s was a crucial one in Sydney. The speed and severity of the changes, if only changes in "understanding," were exemplified by the decision to revise the 1988 Metropolitan Strategy soon after its publication (DoP 1992). The 1988 metropolitan plan came at the very beginning of a growing awareness both of the costs of fringe development and of environmental problems. Although flagging some emerging problems with growth and the potential for more compact development, the 1988 plan's basic premises were firmly behind fringe expansion.

> *The development of new urban areas on Sydney's fringe will ensure the continuing availability of housing for the growing population, especially low-income families who are purchasing their first homes. (DoP 1988, 11)*

> *A population of 3.5 million exerts pressures on the physical environment of a city. Fortunately, many of the environmental problems still experienced in other major cities have been solved for the most part in Sydney, while the air and beaches are relatively unpolluted. (DoP 1988, 27)*

This confidence was short lived. As Gabrielle Kibble, Director of the Department of Planning, announced only three years later:

> *Since the strategy was published a number of significant changes have occurred. These changes include a better understanding of the impact of urban expansion on air and water quality, improved understanding of the cost of developing new sectors and the need to make better use of existing urban areas, changes in the way*

> *employment areas work and the need to take into ac-*
> *count the opportunities presented by surplus govern-*
> *ment sites. (Kibble 1991, n.p).*

Thus Rouse Hill's final planning was conducted in a period of intense questioning of old patterns of development.

> *I suppose it's common in any planning situation that*
> *the plan has probably been prepared sometime in the*
> *past, and the adage that it's immediately out of date*
> *and not representing contemporary expectations. It was*
> *a period I suppose when those expectations were chang-*
> *ing quite rapidly, although [not?] unlike any time in*
> *the past. But once again the planning had not kept up*
> *with community expectations and the approach that the*
> *government was starting to take on urban development.*
> *So you had the regional environmental planning being*
> *done in the mid-eighties. And now the [Water] Board*
> *coming on with the first major bit of infrastructure that's*
> *proposed for that catchment, having to go through a*
> *process that you would normally expect regional plan-*
> *ning to have done at some time in the past. (Andrew,*
> *interview)*

The decision to develop Rouse Hill was not made at one mo-
ment but rather involved a series of incremental actions. The
North West Sector was at first a tentative oval mark on the Sydney
Region Outline Plan, but a mark that meant that people could claim
that the North West Sector had been "planned" since 1968 as, in a
sense, it had been. A series of planning studies and plans strongly
shaped the way the project could be discussed. They kept the focus
on growth. As problems arose with the development someone –
particularly expansionists and developers – came up with a way to
go ahead. Without major disruptions or catastrophes people con-
tinually adjusted to new information and revised the planning in a
partial way, enough to allow Rouse Hill to go on. The timing of the
different problems was crucial to an understanding of Rouse Hill.
Their gradual unfolding, at least up to the 1990s, enabled solutions
to be found one at a time, and undermined opponents' abilities to
paint the development as a disaster.

An increasingly severe set of environmental problems were
resolved by implementing increasingly expensive mitigation

technologies, to the point that the possibility of realizing the development's original purpose of providing a large proportion of its housing to lower-income first-home buyers was uncertain. Although the overall corridor was scaled back in the 1995 metropolitan plan, this was too late to stop the first stage. Once the planning process was locked in it seemed to generate itself, although at any time the absence of funding could have stalled it completely. In this way the formal planning process was partly superseded by the consortium proposal to privately finance and build mandated infrastructure and push the development along. Although constrained and shaped by the planning system, as I show in chapter five, this proposal also reshaped the development to reflect consortium priorities.

End Notes

1   The term "speculator's guide" was quite a common one in planning circles.
2   Local governments were also constrained in their opportunities for comment on plans (e.g. Blacktown City Council 1984, 1987).
3   The project kept a fairly diverse range of consultants occupied throughout the 1980s (e.g. Hirst *et al.* 1989; Howard Tanner and Associates 1984; Kinhill Engineers 1989; Logan and Luscombe 1984; Nesbitt and Donahee 1990; Sinclair Knight Buchanan 1989a, 1989b).
4   Stretton's example is that under a one percent real interest rate a $10 million increase in annual debt service allowed a government to borrow $1000 million, but under an eight percent real interest rate it could only borrow about $130 million for the same increase in annual debt burden (Stretton 1989, xl).
5   These debates were carried out both in journals such as *Urban Policy and Research* and through government sponsored research (e.g. DoP 1990; Hughes Trueman Ludlow 1991; Kirwan 1990; Lang 1990; Murphy and Burnley 1990; Payne 1990; Wilmoth 1990).
6   Much of this concern with water quality actually came from within government (e.g. Burgess no date; DoP 1989b; Camp Scott Furphy and Hawkesbury Agricultural College 1988; DoP 1989b; Water Board 1990; Wilson 1990).
7   The early 1990s was a time of significant work on environmental and infrastructure issues associated with immigration (e.g. Clark *et al.* 1990; Fincher 1991; Murphy *et al.* 1990; National Population Council 1992).
8   One explanation for this process is that immigrants create a demand for housing making it attractive for long-term residents to sell up and relocate to cheaper areas. When overseas migration slows, this demand lessens and fewer people leave Sydney.
9   Frank (1989) reviewed similar studies for the United States concluding that contiguous and medium-density development is less expensive to build

and service that detached housing and non-contiguous growth (see also
Real Estate Research Corporation 1974). These findings have been contested however in methodological terms (e.g. Windsor 1979). Moreover
sprawl is not necessarily expensive in terms of such variables as commuting
time by automobile (Gordon and Wong 1985).

[10] Consolidation scenarios were at densities of 18, 25, 50 and 150 dwelling per
net hectare (including local roads). Fringe development was at lot sizes of
840, 660, 450 and 380 meters squared. Although the authors were vague about
comparing these figures, in an appendix they say a lot size of 500 meters
squared would deliver a density of 20 dwelling per net hectare, a figure that
would seem to ignore local roads as a hectare is 10,000 square meters. In very
rough terms the lower-density consolidation scenarios approximate the smaller
lot sizes (Hughes Trueman Ludlow 1991, iii–iv, appendix D9).

CHAPTER FIVE

Hard and Soft Privatization: Unequal Impacts of Government Withdrawal

The Rouse Hill Infrastructure Consortium (RHIC) involved in physical or "hard" infrastructure, and the Rouse Hill Community Planning Team (RHCPT) dealing with social or "soft" infrastructure, both officially emerged in 1989. The groups were alliances of government and non-government organizations brought together at the instigation of state government bureaucrats as both lobby groups and alternative providers of services. As the development came close to a halt in the mid-1980s because of concerns over costs to government, the two groups – particularly the consortium – provided a means of continuing the project.

The Rouse Hill Infrastructure Consortium, a joint venture between the state Department of Housing and private developers, was exclusively concerned with providing those services critical for state and local government approval of the project. Although subject to an increasingly expensive set of environmental requirements and the focus of a high level of suspicion by other professionals, they seized the initiative in privatizing, gaining a large amount of control over both the form and timing of development. In contrast the Rouse Hill Community Planning Team, a group of non-profit and local government service providers, fought for funding for a set of social services that were not mandated and for which many earlier lower- and middle-income fringe (sub)urban developments were still waiting. The group was the reluctant heir of service privatization.

Privatization allowed this increasingly expensive development to proceed and for the group providing hard infrastructure the result was a net again; they paid for more services but could at least develop their land. Further, for this developer group, as privatization was only partial they still benefited from many government provided services. For the RHCPT, that tended to move toward a consolidationist perspective and whose members were providing social infrastructure, the result was less positive. The increasingly dispersed population became increasingly expensive to service, particularly given service backlogs in earlier fringe developments. The privatization process, then, had different effects on different forms of infrastructure even within Rouse Hill.

Two studies recently published at the time of my initial fieldwork frame these findings. Dear (1989) had examined how privatization was represented in academic writing by planners, noting how particular sectors or perspectives – social planning and social reform – had been marginalized in this privatization debate.[1] As I described in chapter two, Pusey (1991, 41) also found that compared with economic issues, images of society were quite weakly articulated by elite Australian bureaucrats.

However, rather than seeing this marginalization of social concerns as an inevitable outcome of recent privatization policies and economic rationalism, it seems to have a longer history. New-town style urban development throughout the postwar period, and in a number of English-speaking countries, has generally given highest priority to such social services as recreation facilities and shopping, with other facilities being less uniformly available (see Aldridge 1979; Marans and Zehner 1974; Osborn and Whittick 1969). Since the early 1980s state government planning documents had also been telling eloquent stories about the need for social infrastructure in Rouse Hill but had only mandated "hard" infrastructure as a development prerequisite. In Rouse Hill this inequality between hard and soft infrastructure under privatization reflected more than the privatization process itself, drawing on both a longer-lived set of policy priorities favoring physical services as well as a set of underlying differences in the ability to recapture or reallocate money spent on hard and soft infrastructure.

This chapter describes the two coalitions both through their self-representations and the representations of others. Each story deals in turn with the coalition's members, reasons for forming, development through the early 1990s, financing, and political activities. I then analyze their images as consortium and team, their concentrations on physical infrastructure versus community planning, and differences in their power over Rouse Hill. I particularly explore how those involved in Rouse Hill's privatization represented their roles, how these representations were treated by others, and how the power of their representations interacted with other forms of power. For example, while the consortium claimed that its work would provide a broad public benefit, this interpretion was treated with suspicion by many other professionals and activists. The difficulty of finding detailed information about the consortium's activities intensified this suspicion. The Rouse Hill Community Planning Team, in contrast, probably had a more interesting story to tell about the quality of life of the residents of outer suburban areas but lacked the political and economic power to have it heard. Partial privatization also imposed costs on the general public both in terms of continued government expenditure and of reduced openness and accountability. An urban development strategy that reduced the need for suburban expansion may have reduced or limited these costs.

Rouse Hill Infrastructure Consortium

Until the mid 1980s, the practice in urban development in Sydney was that public bodies put in place most physical and social infrastructure in new suburbs. In the late 1980s that practice was challenged. As described in the previous chapter, the high cost of infrastructure made at least some privatization attractive.

In Rouse Hill, the 1986 Draft Regional Environmental Plan estimated state and local government infrastructure costs at AUS$ 2,500 million. By 1989 the estimated cost had risen to $3,090 million or $44,000 per lot, although it was possible some of this could be recovered from developers (DEP 1986b, 81; DoP 1989a, 23). As I explained in chapter four, in 1992 the Water Board released estimates of $53,300 per lot for putting a similar package of physical and social infrastructure in the Rouse Hill area, although increased developer contributions kept the cost to government at $30,000 per lot (see table 2). With these large and growing costs Rouse Hill's planning came close to a halt in 1987.

In March 1988 a Liberal government interested in privatization replaced Labor at the state level (e.g. State Development 1990).

The Rouse Hill Infrastructure Consortium was officially proposed in that year, involving the Department of Housing and other large landowners. The aimed to finance water infrastructure in Rouse Hill as it was the key service required for development approval. The consortium's story shows how a group of powerful public and private sector developers pushed through a privatization proposal where they gained the development initiative and where much of the cost was retained by others parts of government.

At the time of its formal registration as a company in 1989 the RHIC involved AHL Properties and Lauriston Development that owned over 135 hectares, North Sydney Brick and Tile with 385 hectares, and the Department of Housing with over 800 hectares (see chapter one). Other developers joined the group later (see Figure 9).[2] Although most of the Department of Housing's holdings had been bought for public rental housing by the then Housing Commision, by the late 1980s this had been amalgamated with land in the sale program (Land Commission) and the exact split between rental and sale was unclear into the 1990s.

The initial concept behind the Rouse Hill Infrastructure Consortium was to provide funding for and carry out the design, construction, and commissioning of water infrastructure to service the first stage of the Rouse Hill Development Area over a period of approximately 15 years and in 11 or 12 "precincts."[3] The consortium also agreed to contribute a small proportion of the construction cost of major roads, a contribution that in 1989 totaled $440 million (Baulkham Hills Shire Council 1991).

The consortium's investment was attractive to them because keeping land for long periods involved high "holding costs"– the interest payments on loans and the costs of lost opportunities for other investments. By paying for some physical infrastructure their land would be developed earlier than if it had to wait for the Water Board's own timing. This saving in time was a saving in holding costs. In addition, the consortium hoped to build the infrastructure more cheaply by using private sector principles in design and construction. In public explanations the consortium generally expressed its goals in terms of the community benefits of increased land supply and affordability (e.g. Nedeljkovic 1991, 4).

The first stage of the Rouse Hill Development Area involved around 20,000 to 23,000 lots and a potential population of 70,000. Around

Rouse Hill Infrastructure Consortium
    Registered: February 1989
    Principal Activity: Urban Infrastructure Development
    Total value of shares in 1993: $60 (60 shares at $1 each)

Shareholders and Directors (to 1993)
AHL Property (previously Hooker Mercantile and Onmax), 10 shares
    Alan Zammit, Director since July 1990
    Brendan Crotty, Director from March 1989 (also Lauriston)
    Robert Brown, Director March 1989 to July 1990 (also Lauriston)
NSW Land and Housing Corporation (Department of Housing),
10 shares
    Richard Flint, Director from March 1989
    Peter Dransfield, Director from March 1989
    Graham French, Director from November 1991
Graham Trilby, 10 shares
    Bruce Lyon, Director from July 1990
Lauriston Development, 10 shares
    Brendan Crotty, Director from March 1989 (also AHL Property)
    Robert Brown, Director March 1989 to July 1990 (also AHL
    Property)
North Sydney Brick and Tile, 10 shares
    Douglas Lanceley, Director March 1989 to July 1990
    David Magney, Director September 1992 to October 1992
Stocklands (Constructors), 10 shares
    Robert Welsh, Director since July 1990
    Peter Daly, Director since November 1991
Member not on board of RHIC shareholder companies
    Donald Dwyer, Gutteridge, Haskins, Davies, Director March 1989 to
    November 1991

Figure 9   Rouse Hill Infrastructure Consortium Shareholders and Directors
Sources: *Australian Securities Commission (1992, 1993); Department of Housing (1989, 1990, 1991).*

13,200 lots or 42,000 people were in precinct one, the precinct with the most consortium land. The cost of water infrastructure for the first precinct was well over $200 million. This included: water reservoirs and trunk mains for potable (drinking) water and for treated effluent in the innovative dual use system; stage one of the sewage treatment plant including artificial wetlands and riffle zones for high-level tertiary treatment; and various other sewers, mains, and drainage works. Even in the first precinct, however, consortium land was only about one third of developable land (Feizkhah 1994, 12; Manidis Roberts 1991; Zannetides 1991, 1–2, 4–5).

The mechanics of the process were that the consortium, as a non-profit company, would raise money to pay for the approximately $500 million worth of water infrastructure works in the whole of stage one. The consortium would then be repaid in three ways. First, consortium members would pay the consortium for their share of infrastructure at the time of construction (Zannetides 1991, 6). Second, other property developers would continue to pay capital contributions, known as Section 27 contributions, to the consortium via the Water Board at the time of development. Under the consortium arragements these would be calculated to reflect the total cost more exactly than in the past. For those parts of stage one not developed within five years of completion of construction the Water Board agreed to buy the outstanding debt (Feizkhah 1994, 5). In early documents this buyout period was three years (e.g. Nedeljkovic 1991). At this time the Water Board would own and maintain the entire system including that part paid for by the consortium and by earlier Section 27 contributions. The Water Board would be able to pay off some of the remaining debt through further collections of Section 27 contributions, including an interest component, as land was eventually developed (Macquarie Bank 1989, 3; Phelan 1992; Zannetides 1991). Although the consortium's purpose was to have its land developed first, it was in the Water Board's interest to have non-consortium land developed as they would receive consortium contributions whether or not consortium land was developed while non-consortium landowners only paid for infrastructure at the time of development. Although some accounts tried to argue that this deferral arrangement would virtually eliminate the Water Board's financial responsibilities, other accounts from the consortium and Water Board talked only of "significant deferral" and "significant reduction" of Water Board expenses.[4]

The project was widely seen as an example of innovative financing.[5] As a result, the chief executive of the Rouse Hill Infrastructure Consortium was in demand as a speaker at conferences during the early 1990s. As a private venture, however, the consortium was not subject to Freedom of Information regulations and so apart from information released at these (generally expensive) conferences, and brief mentions in rather dispersed reports, the exact details of the financial arrangements between the Water Board and the consortium were not made public in the early 1990s. Further, the agreements with the Water Board were lengthy, complex, and in negotiation for a long time, and so publicly available information was often several years out of date. This lack of public information was an additional cost of privatized development.

Crucial to an assessment of the costs and benefits of privatization, were the various assumptions about rates of development. Of most concern was the consortium's assumption of a high development rate as lower rates would force the Water Board into an expensive buyout. In the early 1980s the maximum development rate in the Rouse Hill Development Area had been set at 3000 to 3500 lots per year based on estimates of private development at 1000 lots per year, and Department of Housing production at 1000 lots of public housing and 1000 lots for sale. It also took into account Water Board, local government, and human service capacities (DEP 1986b, 17–18; DoP 1988, 47). A figure of 2000 lots was seen as more achievable (Searle 1984, n.p). These 3000 and 2000 lot figures were used by the consortium (e.g. Macquarie Bank 1989, 3). The consortium idea was floated in a very buoyant residential property market. In Sydney, house prices rose 19 percent in 1987 and 41 percent in 1988, a gain that contrasted favorably with the 1987 stock market crash (Wood and Bushe-Jones 1991, 13; Boylen 1991).

In 1988 a study prepared for the Department of Housing, however, found that development rates in single areas (or "fronts") in Sydney were generally around 300 lots per year, one-tenth of the estimated production at Rouse Hill, with "little scope for substantially increasing development rates" (Cardew 1988, 61). In 1990 and 1991, the Indicative Planning Council for the Housing Industry – a joint public-private organization – estimated lot production in Rouse Hill at betwen 900 and 1800 lots per year with the higher figure described as "optimistic" (DITAC 1990, 65–66; see also DITAC 1991, 57). The worldwide recession of the early 1990s also affected this residential property market significantly, making investment in residential property less attractive to both large investors and individual home buyers and making even 2000 lots per year seem a high figure.

These different analyses had important implications for the relative risks to the consortium and other parts of government. At lower development rates the cost to the Water Board of its commitment to buy out the consortium after five years could be very high. Although the consortium paid for the infrastructure on its land at the time of construction, consortium land was not a majority of land in the Rouse Hill Development Area. As the consortium was in control of infrastructure construction and phasing, members were in a good position to market their land quickly. If development was slower than 3000 lots per year, or even the 2000 lot alternative scenario, it was likely that the undeveloped lots would not belong to those in the consortium. However, it was these non-consortium lots that were costly to the Water Board as it had to pay for the infrastructure servicing them after five years while not collecting payments for the infrastructure until the land was developed. In a worst case scenario, a low development rate would leave little non-consortium land developed and the Water Board footing the bill for the majority of the Rouse Hill Development Area infrastructure. This was an improvement over the situation where the Water Board financed all infrastructure up front. However, without the consortium's pressure Rouse Hill may have been kept on hold much longer also deferring Water Board expenditures in this expensive-to-develop area, particularly as serviced land was available in other parts of the Sydney region.

While quite technical, and often buried in reports and submissions that were not widely distributed, enough of this discussion circulated to reinforce a more general perception that the Department of Housing in alliance with private developers had devised the consortium arrangement to reduce the DoH's own (holding) costs. The Department of Housing pursued this goal even though the resulting urban growth would mean greater expense to other departments and to the government as a whole. They refused to budge from an outdated metropolitan planning process, a process that favored growth.

Consortium members certainly used their financial power and government connections to ensure development continued, including putting the local governments under pressure to work quickly and threatening them with a loss of planning powers. As two local government employees remarked:

> *We were under enormous pressure to deal with all these issues and we [were] aware of the state government being an important player and stakeholder in the whole exercise and the pressure being exerted by the consortium. I don't think any one of those players will deny that there was pressure being exerted because there was. (Edward, interview)*
>
> *[The state government] keep[s] on telling us we've got to be financially responsible, we've got to assess the financial implications of all the planning we do. Yet we were forced into doing this, really railroaded and threatened with loss of planning powers and goodness knows what if we didn't put through the [local rezoning] plan. (Eric, interview)*

The consortium's own financial arrangements remained unclear during the recession of the early 1990s, but by late 1992 financing had been organized from a syndicate of banks to build and commission the sewage treatment plant (Phelan 1992). However, in 1993 the Water Board publicly acknowledged that it did "not know what the services would cost in the long term" (Southern 1993a, 4; 1993b).

In terms of preliminary estimates of development rates, residents started moving in during 1994. Development rates were around 500 per year in year one (1993–1994) and 600 in the second year with 1000 per year expected over the next five years. However, with the property market in a slump it was unlikely to reach 1000 lots per year very quickly (Cardew 1997). In addition, local officials worried that the consortium was only putting in minimal physical infrastructure in the early precincts, necessitating augmentation if the development took off (RHCPT Minutes, 17 February 1994).

Issues of finance were not only problems faced by the consortium in developing its water infrastructure. Changes in the regulation of pollution sources had a significant influence, increasing the cost of anti-pollution technologies in the sewerage and drainage systems.

Certain design features of the water infrastructure, including the decision to have one large sewage treatment plant, were inherited by the consortium that was then forced into finding increasingly sophisticated technical fixes for the problems that arose from these decisions. This occurred even as many greener elements of the Water Board questioned these fixes and the development as a whole.[6]

The story of the consortium is thus the story of a partnership between private developers and a pro-development government department proposing privatization as a way of dealing with the high up-front costs of new development. While there were alternatives to development, with the help of Joe Schipp, the powerful Minister of Housing in the Liberal-National Party government, the consortium was able to override these objections. However, many state and local government agencies and officials expressed concern at being forced into paying for a large number of physical and social services in the mixed-income housing area. Others were also worried about the overall costs to government. As one local government professional explained:

> We had the state government election in May [1991] and the most notable decision, from our point of view, that happened after that was the Minister for the Water Board became [the same person as] the Minister for Housing. And it was only I think a week after the [election]... that these insurmountable problems with the plant had been sorted out and the plant was given an approval. Otherwise no housing could have occurred. And it's our cynical view that the Department of Housing's probably won yet again and they'll get what they want, when they want, where they want. (Eric, interview)

Rouse Hill Community Planning Team

The second public-private alliance operating in Rouse Hill – the Rouse Hill Community Planning Team – was formed in 1989 shortly after the consortium was registered. The story of the RHCPT is of a group struggling to define its role in the development within a context of quite limited resources.

Over the years a number of interdepartmental working groups, Department of Planning officers, and local government groups had come up with an evolving list of "baseline" human services for the Rouse Hill area.[7] The Rouse Hill Human Services Working Group, an interdepartmental committee formed in late 1988, "identified that non-government agencies could also play a major role in providing adequate services" (Notes. ... 1989, n.p.; Green 1988). Following a seminar called by the Department of Planning in September 1989, the Rouse Hill Community Planning Team was formed as a planning and advocacy group for human service providers (RHCPT 1992b, 1).

Rouse Hill Community Planning Team meetings included local government officers and non-government groups such as churches, the Boy Scouts, the Red Cross, organizations serving immigrants, and public health groups. Government bodies were classed as "resource" members of the team while non-government groups were classed as full members. Representatives from federal government community service agencies, and from the offices of members of state parliament, attended from time to time. Some members of the group were from the local area, but others represented metropolitan-wide organizations; the organizers of the initial seminar were particularly interested in increasing the level of knowledge about the Rouse Hill area for these city-wide groups.

The goals of the group were reformulated several times. By 1992 the team had reached a succinct statement, that they were involved in: "informing the community of what was taking place in the region; and advocating on behalf of future residents in the North West Sector for the timely, adequate an appropriate provision of community services" (RHCPT 1992b, 1; Southam 1992). These aims reflected team members' experiences working in the local area and dealing with the problems of earlier land releases.

From an initial emphasis on individual organizations coming together to further their separate concerns, the group developed toward an interest and involvement in larger issues including infrastructure finance, transport, and public health. This interest in broader issues, however, caused many on the team to question the whole development, leading to a series of intense discussions. The issue was a difficult one. As the Rouse Hill Community Planning Team members learned more about the Rouse Hill development they became more uneasy about it. They worried that transportation would be underfunded and this would lead to social isolation.

They were concerned about the public health impacts of building in an area with high smog levels. However, the evidence that produced this sense of unease frequently took a long time to understand and was often in areas – environmental standards, state government finance – in which their organizations had no expertise. Even if they protested the development they were unlikely to stop it. Even if the development was stopped many of their organizations would need to provide services for the same increase in population in another location, although locations in established areas would have some existing services to build upon and would not need as many new buildings. While many team members felt that the Rouse Hill development could have negative social consequences, they felt that persuading their organizations to oppose the development was impossible. The team finally decided that while many of its members did not support Rouse Hill's development as individuals, they needed to be pragmatic and represent their organizations in making human service provision in Rouse Hill as effective as possible (e.g. RHCPT Minutes 21 October 1991, 21 May 1992).

Crucial for the team was the apparent lack of government or consortium commitment to providing a set of basic human services they could then augment. In its early planning the Department of Environment and Planning had included both community services and physical infrastructure in its list of "basic services on new housing estates" (DEP 1986b, 15; DEP 1984a, 211–213). However, none of the planning documents specified how human services would be funded. Moreover, the legal instrument of the Regional Environmental Plan tied development approval by local governments to the provision of only some of these "basic" services: "water, sewerage, drainage and power" leading to the consortium's focus (DoP 1989a, 28).

Thus physical services, dubbed "hard infrastructure" in development circles, had priority over "soft infrastructure" or human services. The division between infrastructure as engineering and earthmoving, with large budgets and workforces dominated by men, and infrastructure based in interpersonal skills, with smaller budgets and workforces dominated by women or by men in caring professions, was also reflected in the state budgetary process (Connell 1990, 524; Masterplan Consultants 1987, 20–21). Of public utilities needed in Rouse Hill, electricity and water were both provided "off-budget" where the supplier of the service, although part of the government, was an agency that charged for its services and was mainly funded by user charges and not from general tax revenues. Telephone was at that time provided by a federal government corporation, gas by a private company, waste disposal by local councils, and so none of these represented a drain on state government funds. Although the state had committed itself to an"intermediate" transport corridor to Rouse Hill's regional commercial center, most probably a bus right-of-way, buses in the area would be privately operated. Only roads, traditionally provided by state government in the case of arterial roads, presented a large initial drain on the state budget. However, not until the early 1990s, when the state roads authority began to suffer cutbacks, did road provision become a major problem (e.g. Department of Transport 1992).

While most physical infrastructure was either self-financing or not provided by the state level of government, this was not the case for social infrastructure. In Rouse Hill, early suggestions that the state government should buy up land and use the profits from commercial land development and from land rezoning to pay for human services were rejected (DEP 1984b, 21). Thus community service financing involved potentially difficult transfers of resources from one area to another within the state government. However, as the transfers did not need to be made until planning was far progressed and populations about to arrive, they had little influence on the initial decision to develop (Masterplan Consultants 1987, 21).

Although human service funding sources were not clearly stated in any of the plans, costs were gradually released. In a 1992 document the state Department of Community Services (DCS) estimated that over 15 years its community services in Rouse Hill would cost a total of around $25.3 million for capital works and $127.4 million for recurrent funding (DCS 1992, n.p.). Given that the statewide recurrent budget for the Department of Community Services was about one-tenth of either Education or Health, this Department of Community Service costing was presumably only a small part of the total human services budget. Although much of the human service budget was tied to population alone, capital costs were related to urban expansion.

Problems of human service funding were exacerbated by the large backlogs in servicing areas of western Sydney developed in the 1970s and 1980s (DoP 1988, 23, 47). The consortium proposal, involving a very fragmented land release pattern on four "fronts", merely reinforced this problem. (The use of "front" was quite confusing in this debate as the Rouse Hill Development Area was often considered one or two fronts in terms of housing markets but four fronts in terms of human service provision.) As the RHCPT stated publicly, Rouse Hill was "on the fringe of the fringe" (RHCPT 1992b, 3).

Although there were numerical standards for human service provision, with the exception of school education these were generally ignored. Part of the team's strategy was thus to attempt to make human service standards more binding, to create a firm "baseline." As team members discussed in one general meeting:

> *John: ... If Sydney has to grow, let's do it the best way. This team doesn't have to get caught up with the juggernaut of the western suburbs.*
>
> *Oliver: [The environmentalist who had talked to the group at a previous meeting] let us off the hook, as if everything is done well the development could go ahead. The problem is it probably won't be done well in areas like transport and water. And from our perpective, looking at the backlog estates, we can warn about the problems that could be avoided. And we need to draw a line, a baseline below which we can't accept the development.*
>
> *Sam: I wasn't here last week but does anyone here really believe we're in a position to stop things and go back to ground level?*
>
> *Maria: I don't think we have to look at it like that but we need to bring pressure to bear. And unless we think we have some influence we may as well go home.*
>
> *Sam: I think the influence we have is that it's the first time we're in before the development is.*
>
> *Oliver: ... We have influence if we get our facts straight, and concentrate where our expertise is.*
>
> *Laura: ... We can have a significant part in the whole picture.*

*Matthew: I'm Matthew from [a federal government
human service agency]. We're interested to get in at
the ground floor into the area, [in a way that is] suitable for the community. And unless there's a strong
voice at the outset community services could stay at a
mediocre level.
(Meeting Q, notes)*

Obviously, creating a baseline was not their only strategy. In their
very next statements several other areas of influence were raised:
alliances, the timing of their own investments, and knowledge in
their areas of expertise.

Supplementing these strategies the Rouse Hill Community Planning Team members tried to do what the scientific environmentalists had done, argue for their planning interests in economic terms.
This strategy of arguing in economic terms has a long history in
Australia (see Sandercock 1990, 67). The team searched for studies of the long-term economic costs of failing to provide human
services in an adequate and timely manner, but studies of human
services tended to be anecdotal or based on non-economic measures like user satisfaction.[8] Further, the team did not have
the expertise, resources, or time to undertake this kind of research.
Making human services seem critical was a difficult task in
the face of the compellingly argued and quantifiable economic
and environmental problems facing western Sydney and the
government's history of emphasizing physical infrastructure.

The data problem spurred the team to develop its own "dos-
sier" or information package for use when members approached
politicians and bureaucrats, stressing the long-team problems of
inadequate human service provision. It was the basis of a public
meeting held in October 1992 with approximately 70 people at-
tending (RHCPT 1992a, 1992b).

By 1993 the group decided its mission was clear enough to consider holding a joint public meeting with local progress associations and with environmental groups – organizations that the team
might disagree with but who also represented the "community"
(RHCPT Minutes, 16 June 1993). The group was still meeting in
1998, working on baselines, networking with other groups, attend-
ing state-level meetings, and meeting the new residents.

Consorting and Teamwork

The previous sections have sketched out the histories and activities of the RHIC and RHCPT. The rest of the chapter compares the two groups in terms of their public representations, using this to assess the mixed impacts of privatization on issues such as accountability, responsiveness, and government spending.

The Rouse Hill Infrastructure Consortium and the Rouse Hill Community Planning Team, although in many ways occupying fundamentally different roles in Rouse Hill, still shared some characteristics. The catalyst for both coalitions came from public servants concerned about continuing policies in the context of decreasing government funds for development. In the case of the RHIC the instigators were bureaucrats at a high level in the Department of Housing interested in continuing low-density suburban growth in areas where they owned land. For the RHCPT the instigators were middle-level professionals concerned with planning for, and providing, human services. These bureaucrats formed the groups to become external power bases maintaining pressure on the state government to promote fringe urban development and to provide human services in new areas. The groups were more than external power bases, however, in that they were in the position to actually take over government responsibilities in those areas where it was clear that government had withdrawn or wanted to withdraw: water infrastructure, and some social services.

These privatization moves were, however, partial. The consortium included a government department and water infrastructure developed by the consortium would eventually be owned and operated by the Water Board. In addition, the move to "up-front" payments was arguably not so different from the previous rating (taxing) system. Many Rouse Hill Community Planning Team members were at least partly government funded and some of the services they were advocating had rarely been provided in a timely manner by government and so their absence could not strictly be called privatization.

Privatization was, however, important in Rouse Hill. Without the Rouse Hill Infrastructure Consortium, Rouse Hill may well have remained stalled in the planning process, halted by a lack of funds. The Rouse Hill Community Planning Team was potentially an innovative way to ensure that a network of non-government human services was put in place in a timely and coordinated manner. Although the groups had very different levels of commitment to the idea of Rouse Hill, on some level they performed similar functions.

The coalitions' names reflect this pattern of basic similarity along with some differences. In Australian usage a team is "a number of persons associated in some joint action." Meanwhile a consortium, is 1." a combination of financial institutions, capitalists, etc., for carrying into effect some financial operation requiring large resources of capital. 2. an association or union" (*Concise Macquarie Dictionary*). Thus the meaning of team and the second definition of consortium – as association – are virtually interchangeable. However, the differences in their names were also striking and affected public perceptions.

Most dramatically, the Rouse Hill Infrastructure Consortium bred conspiracy theories through its name: "I think that generally there is a suspicion of consortiums. I think that people don't understand what that name means. If it's a consortium, people are consorting to get [other] people" (Susan, interview). There was a general perception of "the consortium being like the Mafia" (Dora, interview).

This perception was based on a number of factors including the difficulty of finding public information. Several setbacks to consortium members also provoked distrust. Part of the Hooker group, that included two consortium members, filed for bankruptcy in 1989.[9] The administrative culture of the Department of Housing also promoted widespread suspicion that came to a head in 1992. The final report of the Royal Commission into Productivity in the Building Industry in NSW, named the "Gyles Report," concluded of the Department:

> It is difficult to imagine a sorrier tale of administrative incompetence, if not worse than that, which emerges from the combined impact of looking through these external windows into the operation of the Department [of Housing].
>
> The Department controls the spending of more than $300 million of public money per annum. It is obvious that it is impervious to criticism, no matter how damning. It appears to be beyond internal reconstruction. It

also appears that it is beyond control by the rest of the
Executive Government. (Gyles 1992, 86)

The Director of the Department of Housing, Richard Flint, resigned
soon after the report was released, although he remained on the
RHIC Board. Following the resignation of the state Premier in mid-
1992 over another scandal, the Department was given to the Minister for Planning in the new cabinet (Coultan 1992). Previously
the Minister for Housing had been senior to the Minister for Planning in cabinet and thus able to push his own agenda. A subsequent external inquiry recommended reconstructing the Department of Housing, contracting out many funtions and regionalizing
others (Mant 1992).

Even before 1992, however, the actions of the Department of
Housing had provoked criticism. The Department of Housing was
generally perceived as a property developer rather than an organization working in the public interest (e.g. NSW 1990–1991,
447, 27 February). The vast majority of the land held by the Department of Housing had originally belonged to the Housing
Commission (over 600 hectares) and was originally intended for
public housing. The amalgamation of the Housing and Land Com-
missions in the new Department of Housing in 1986 allowed this
land to be pooled. By the 1990s, although the exact figures were
not released, the majority was targeted for sale by the Housing
Department's trading arm, Landcom. While most people agreed
that old-style, large, homogenous, inaccessible, fringe-suburban
public housing estates should be avoided, and Landcom targeted
the lower and middle sections of the ownership market, this was
still a significant move toward the privatization of space. It reinforced the image of the Department of Housing as a private developer plotting for its own ends.

In the early 1990s, conspiracy theories also focused on the Liberal government that had approved the consortium plan. In fact the
group behind the consortium included people with contacts in both
Liberal and Labor parties, but there was room for concern about
the business and bureaucratic elites involved in urban development.
Michael Eyers, who had a role in arranging financing in the early
period of the consortium, was a member of the Land Commission
under Labor and was appointed as Head of the Department of
Housing from 1986 to 1988 by a state Labor government. Macquarie

Bank, which prepared some early documents for the Rouse Hill
Infrastructure Consortium, had Liberal Party connections
(Macquarie Bank 1989). John Hewson, the Leader of the federal
Liberal Opposition in the early 1990s, had been on the board of
directors of the bank until 1987 (Australian Securities Commis-
sion 1992).
Other individuals active in forming the Rouse Hill Infrastruc-
ture Consortium were prominent property developers. Brendan
Crotty, from the Hooker group, sat on the National Home Builders
Council of the Housing Industry Association, the group that produced a major report *Housing Towards 2000* (HIA 1990). Peter
Dransfield was the first Department of Housing Director under the
Liberals in 1988, and returned to his private development firm
without relinquishing his seat on the consortium board. These elite
connections fed the suspicions of other professionals about the consorting aspect of the consortium.
The consortium members were aware of these suspicions, publicly blaming it on poor communication and lack of trust. As one
explained in an interview:

> *I think there's a fundamental distrust by the govern-*
> *ment of the private sector. And again I'm not talking*
> *about senior levels of government, I'm talking about*
> *further down the line. And that's not in relation to Rouse*
> *Hill, it's a general thing. ... In most of the negotiations*
> *that we've had with government we've had a lot of*
> *agreement, a lot of cooperation, at the senior manage-*
> *ment levels. [But] once it gets below those levels you*
> *end up with this fundamental distrust, or I guess an*
> *attitude of "if they want to do this deal there must be*
> *something in it for them that we can't see" or "they*
> *must be trying to get something out of this that we're*
> *not aware of." And that's just not the case. (Timothy,*
> *interview)*

In contrast the "team" in the Rouse Hill Community Planning
Team's name evoked images of sporting teams or perhaps bureaucratic work groups, forms of association that were relatively in-
nocuous as well as powerless. This was a connotation that the team
members would have, perhaps unhappily, seen as relatively accurate. Compared with the elites in the consortium the RHCPT were

generally at a middle level in large organizations or the heads of local groups. However, the RHCPT's focus was not primarily on the character of their association, but on the substance of their, interest, "Community Planning."

Community and Infrastructure

The word "Community," in the name of the Rouse Hill Community Planning Team, stood for several overlapping elements of its mission. The Rouse Hill Community Planning Team claimed, as its first aim, "to represent the future population of the Rouse Hill area," the future community (RHCPT Minutes, 21 November 1991). Community-based groups from the local area, local governments, and city-wide community service organizations, combined to speak for the people who would move to Rouse Hill. This use of the term community was obviously open to debate as there was really some question about who the future population would be, why the Rouse Hill Community Planning Team were legitimate representatives of that future population, and whether people choosing to move to the fringe even wanted community services.

Further, the characteristics of the eventual residents of Rouse Hill changed as development costs increased, the mix of housing became more diverse to meet consolidation targets, and calls for scaling back development made its size uncertain. The gradual shift, or the gradual realization by the RHCPT of a shift, from lower- and middle-income first-home buyers to a higher end of the market, mixed with some public housing, was hard for the team to assimilate into their ideas about needs. Many in the group worked in the Blacktown local government area, the site of public housing developments with thousands of units, along with owner-occupied housing traditionally inhabited by young families. Although by US standards the areas were physically attractive, dominated by detached houses and townhouses, these demographic characteristics created a distinct set of human service requirements. Many RHCPT members were set up to deal with those requirements.

The state government initially added to the confusion by giving out ambiguous information about the future population. The 1989 Regional Environmental Plan started its section on human services with the statement: "Many residents in new housing areas are young families," presumably with lower incomes (DoP 1989a, 10). In the same document, however, a second section on human services stated that the "first areas to be developed within the initial release area" would help "overcome the perceived shortage of high priced land" (DoP 1989a, 17).

Overall the team's constituency was uncertain. It was a difficult constituency to lobby for, and it was also potentially very expensive to service as those who managed to provide services like churches and scout halls ahead of demand risked paying for largely empty buildings if development was delayed or dipersed, or if the demographics changed still further. In the long, slow process of developing Rouse Hill, they were at a distinct disadvantage.

In contrast "Infrastructure," the term indicating the area of concern for the Rouse Hill Infrastructure Consortium, seemed a far more technical term than community. As it could connote either "hard" (physical) or "soft" (social) infrastructure there was a measure of ambiguity, but in its public statements the consortium made it clear that its focus was "hard."

Privatization and Planning

Neither the consortium nor the RHCPT were particularly happy about infrastructure privatization as both would have preferred more government subsidies and even government provision. Perhaps the main groups involved in Rouse Hill to be positive about privatization, apart from some disciples of Milton Friedman sitting far off in state and federal treasury departments, were the various sorts of environmentalists opposed to the development. Local environmentalists interested in protecting the visual character of their residential area from suburban encroachment saw privatization as a way of pricing others out. Those interested in regional and global environmental issues saw privatization as a way of making an increasingly affluent group of outer suburban residents pay the cost of sprawl. The consortium, however, was better placed than others in terms of political contacts, policy context, and economic resources to shape the character and extent of privatization to suit their own needs. The consortium took the lead in designing the privatization arrangements. The Department of Housing had a strong minister at the time of the proposal giving them a clear voice in the highest levels of state government.

In the 1990s, then, privatization allowed parts of the state government committed to 1960s-style suburban expansion to continue this practice at Rouse Hill, also benefiting some parts of the private sector. The Department of Housing, in particular, was able to push its agenda although at some cost to other parts of government as well as to itself. In contrast, the human service providers in the RHCPT had the difficult job of reacting to, and to some extent paying for, others' decisions. However, human services had rarely been high on the planning and development agenda. The state government had set up the system that made water infrastructure the key component needed for development to go ahead, and that had marginalized human service funding even in the pre-privatization days.

This analysis raises at least two issues: that partial privatization continued and even generated a number of public costs of urban development; and that in terms of minimizing the human and monetary costs of development, changing the character of development may have been more successful than changing the way it was financed.

First, in Rouse Hill the structure of mandates did not keep up with the structure of privatization, and so property developers, and pro-development government departments, could take advantage of this mismatch. Thus a relatively small private, or departmental, investment in mandated infrastructure could leverage large commitments in terms of other government provided physical and social services. Without privatization, the state government may have looked for other options apart from low-density expansion, options that reduced its overall costs. It may have thus avoided large capital investments in facilities such as roads and human services, using excess capacity in existing urban areas and in other fringe locations.

Privatization not only continued these direct government costs but actually generated another set of public costs to do with responsiblility and openness, for example the consortium's exemption from Freedom of Information requirements and its lack of accountability to the wider public. These were combined with the probable under-provision of social services in the area to provide an interlocking set of human costs that were omitted from privatization balance sheets.

Second, privatization of infrastructure provision – through consortium-style arrangements and increased user fees – was only one option for decreasing infrastructure costs to government. The other main alternative was consolidation that would cut down the need for fringe development. As I described in chapter four, a Department of Planning study of four areas including Rouse Hill, had found that savings occurred under a variety of fringe lot size and consolidation density scenarios. These calculations omitted the counterbalancing subsidies to central locations – where such facilities as large sporting and entertainment facilities were located – but did seem to indicate that alternatives to suburban expansion could provide significant overall savings.

Thus in Rouse Hill the property developers providing physical infrastructure generally won the battle to shape the development's services, although only after several decades and with an uncertain future given the likelihood that environmental regulations will increase costs still further if future stages go ahead. Their public arguments were rather weak rationalizations of pursuing their own interests, however their interests were also a continuation of a long-term state-government policy supporting growth as popular and egalitarian. The human service providers generally lost, but even in the pre-privatization days their position had been weak. There was little money for state government provided human services in the 1990s, but the situation had been similar in previous decades. There was not a clear way to articulate social needs beyond the local level and even good public arguments could not override the absence of a mandate for human services.

End Notes

[1] In planning, writing on privatization has focused on a variety of strategies from load shedding and contracting out to increased user fees, demand management, and public-private partnerships (see Frieden and Sagalyn 1989; Kirwan 1990; NHS 1991d; Payne 1990; Squires 1989; Wilmoth 1990). In public policy studies authors have examined the uneven patterns of privatization policies over geographic space and through time (Richardson *et al.* 1992; Stubbs and Barnett 1992). The varied institutional frameworks of the shadow state have also been a focus in planning scholarship (Mallett 1993; Stoker 1987).

2   The private developers Stocklands Constructors and Graham Trilby also joined
      the base consortium group (see Figure 9). The consortium's technical advisors,
      the consulting firm Gutteridge Haskins Davies (GHD), were initially repre-
      sented on the board. In 1989 property developers Mirvac Limited and Leighton
      had paid subscriptions for provisional membership (Macquarie Bank 1989,
      3). A deed or agreement between the RHIC and the Water Board was signed in
      1990, although negotiations continued (NSW 1990–1991, 7751).

3   One of the difficulties in examining the consortium's proposal was the contra-
      dictory information that was given out, in this case over the number of precincts
      (Nedeljkovic 1991, 8; Macquarie Bank 1989, 4; and Zannetides 1991, 1).

4   Those arguing for virtual elimination included the Macquarie Bank (1989, 5)
      and the Water Board (1992, 18); those for significant reduction included
      Nedeljkovic (1991, 9–10) and Zannetides (1991, 6).

5   The project was quite a hot topic in 1991 and 1992 (see DHHCS 1992b, 70;
      Department of Industry, Technology and Commerce [DITAC] 1991, 74; Kirwan
      1991, 13–14; National Population Council 1992, 70–71).

6   Those questioning development in western Sydney included Wilson (1990)
      and the Water Board (1991b,7; c.f. Water Board 1985). Technical fixes, such
      as the use of recycled water, were not only expensive in themselves but required
      quite a bit of advertising and education (e.g. RHIC 1993, 1992–94).

7   There were a number of such baselines (e.g. DEP 1986b; Department of Family
      and Community Services 1990; Nesbitt and Donahee 1990).

8   Australian studies were mostly case studies of problems with provision (Dalton
      1980; Sarkissian and Doherty 1987; see also Land 1990, 91). Studies from the
      US were generally older (Burby et al. 1975; Zehner 1977).

9   The two consortium members in the Hooker group were AHL Property and
      Lauriston Development.

CHAPTER SIX

Urban Development and the Power of Ideas

This book has given an account, or rather several accounts, of Rouse Hill and of the ideas about urban form that helped to shape it. It focused on a period, the early 1990s, when suburban form was being actively reinterpreted. The study revolved around two concerns: how ideas, perspectives, or frameworks about urban form were constructed or articulated; and the effects of these ideas on (plans for) Rouse Hill. It approached these questions by telling the story of Rouse Hill in four ways. First, it described the conversations between several frameworks that groups involved in Rouse Hill used to interpret the project and envision its future. Second, it outlined and critiqued some of the metaphors or images that helped focus and represent public and professional discussions about the project. Third, it explored the formal planning process and a series of emerging problems, a situation at once highly structured yet open to external influences and manipulation. Fourth, the volume examined moves toward privatization, focusing on two public-private coalitions diverging significantly in their scope of influence.

Although presented separately as a way of highlighting the multiple processes at work in a large urban development, these stories about Rouse Hill were interdependent. Members of coalitions interpreted the project through some of the five frameworks, working within and around the formal planning process, and articulating their positions to others as images rather than causal arguments. The various ways of telling the story of Rouse Hill also dealt with many of the same substantive issues – air pollution, water quality, privatization – although with some stark differences in emphasis and approach. In talking and writing about Rouse Hill people drew on a set of public and professional debates about the future of cities, and some of their actions in turn influenced these wider conversations.

While Rouse Hill exists in a specific location as both a pile of earth and a proposed urban development corridor, the issues its development raises reach beyond the specifics of this location. Changes in the economy and the natural environment, activist challenges to professional expertise, moves to privatize infrastructure, and debates over urban form and urban growth, are common to many cities, not only Sydney. In this chapter I return to my original discussion about urban form and action, examining how professionals and activists faced these changes and how they dealt with those who saw the situation differently.

This chapter is organized in three parts. First, it examines how ideas shaped the character of urban form at Rouse Hill. Some ideas spoke powerfully to contemporary concerns, provided a resonant interpretation of the present and a compelling vision of the future, and gave some power to those who lacked administrative and economic clout. The second section analyzes how groups claimed to speak for a wide set of public concerns, what they called the total picture or balanced view, through fairly stripped down representations. Groups, however, interpreted their areas of concern and responsibility — in terms of people and issues — quite differently. One group's breadth was another's bias. In the third section I outline some tensions between the kinds of issues and communities the different groups felt responsible to and for, and the often different scope of their job descriptions. Planners in particular were expected by themselves and others to have a wide area of concern or control, although their actual professional role was quite limited.

People and Ideas

Although high-level actors – directors of major development companies, cabinet members, bankers, and heads of government departments – have the ability to approve, encourage, or stop major developments, this study concentrated on another group. These were middle-class, middle-level professionals and activists, people with some influence on plans for the Rouse Hill Development Area. They included urban planners in a variety of institutional settings as well as a number of others performing overlapping coordinating and research functions or seeing themselves as having a vision that should be taken into account: people such as environmental activists and bureaucrats, and human service professionals. These people exercised their influence through a number of mechanisms: making and approving policies, planning and designing developments, helping shape the climate of ideas about urban form, or opposing or acquiescing to particular development components or strategies.

A limited but reasonably diverse range of publicly articulated frameworks on urban form were evident in Rouse Hill. Each was constructed like a collage, drawing from a variety of sources – interests, generation, gendered family experiences, housing histories, immigration and travel experiences, professional roles – and often involving different interpretations of quite similar characteristics or evidence. All had qualities admired by a variety of people. Expansionists retained a stubborn commitment to providing high-quality housing for the middle and working classes. Developers did the complex work of producing serviced land and houses. Scientific environmentalists were thoughtful advocates for the natural world. Local environmentalists wanted to protect their lifestyle that brought them close to nature, and other locals hoped to make the best of the metropolitan planning decisions to urbanize their semi-rural environment. Consolidationists tried to respond to social, environmental, and economic change with an urban form emphasizing the city's vitality.

I stress these admirable qualities because in the planning of Rouse Hill, as in many other planning situations, groups took strong stands and tended to ignore or dismiss opponents. Participants easily asserted their truth against other's biases. Stressing their admirable qualities does not imply that they were all equally correct, however, rather that they were all somehow important for understanding Rouse Hill, and debates over growth more generally. They in some sense contained a truth, if much else besides (see Bernstein 1976, xx).

For some the strength of these frameworks and images was crucial, for others less so. For example, developers had both access to capital and high-level government contacts and so the persuasive power of their ideas — at least to more general audiences – was less important than for other groups. Persuading bankers, politicians, and elite bureaucrats — and legitimating their actions to a wider public — were important tasks, but they could call upon other resources to maintain the momentum of the project. For others ideas were vital. By writing much of their vision into Rouse Hill's initial planning expansionists had defined the discretionary space of planners coming after them. In the 1990s, however, they had to fight to maintain this framework in the face of enviromental criticisms and privatization moves. Local environmentalists tried to use the persuasive power of their ideas to create some opportunities to oppose the development beyond formal objections to plans, for example trying to gain press coverage.[1]

Public Interests and Rationality

By claiming that their views were balanced, rational, or holistic, and accusing others of bias or oversimplification, those involved in Rouse Hill seemed to need some public recognition that their position was common and correct. That is, their positions were based on good reasons that all sensible people either did agree with, or would agree with if they considered the situation seriously. In the dispersed and ritualized planning process of Rouse Hill these positions tended to be asserted by groups against each other with little room for compromise. This situation is in some contrast with Innes' (1996) account of the possibilities of consensus building in large projects, a process that relies on a much more interactive form of planning than occurred at Rouse Hill.

The following quotations from a scientific environmentalist and developer are just one example of the claims and accusations that abounded in Rouse Hill.

> *In the next few years when Sydney finds out how short a supply of land it has and the pressures are on to keep those, to even just to maintain supply, I think the issue's going to turn around and become more of a "how do we house these people" type issue, rather than "how are we going to prevent development."*
>
> *And out of that I see a nicely balanced approach to development where for years the developer had it his own way, rape and pillage the trees and that sort of thing, and knock everything down. And then all of a sudden the environmental movement's had it all its way*

over the last few years. And I expect that pendulum to swing back and some balanced arguments being put. In fact, I read in the paper the other day someone putting the argument that the environmental movement has got to really start to look at itself and start to be a little more responsible and not just simply say no to everything, and to look for alternate solutions as the development industry has had to do. (Gregory, developer, interview)

You see this is the narrow-mined view that developers keep taking. They're only concerned with their development. They don't look at what's happening on a catchment-wide basis. If you keep closing down market gardens time and time again where are you going to put them? Who's going to supply who? Are you going to contribute to, if you're going to shut down your local markets then you're going to have to start importing, your [national] deficit gets bigger. (Roger, scientific environmentalist, interview)

The approach that we take is really holistic and we give the best advice taking into account all the factors. Whereas if you go through... the Environmental Impact Statement, I don't want to single out Rouse Hill here, but just from my knowledge, they're always biased. They're biased because it's the way the process works. (Roger, scientific environmentalist, interview)

Groups made similar claims to representing truth or breadth – it seemed to be important to have a wider view or perhaps a public interest – but had quite different ideas about the content of those positions.

These were generally modernist positions, of the kind of complex multifaceted modernism Berman (1988) so elegantly describes. Some were captivated by the more quantifiable aspects of the development's impact on nature; others were concerned about issues like equality, liberty, and justice for individuals, families, and other groups; some worried about both (Harper and Stein 1995, 234). From the outside the situation certainly had elements of various postmodern positions: a lack of shared foundations, some incommensurability or lack of shared premises, an anti-dualistic refusal to separate fact from value, and multiple claims to truth (Moore Milroy 1991; Harvey 1996). From the inside, however, while there was a certain acceptance that people held different viewpoints, most people thought their position was closest to the truth and should win out if only everyone else would look at things logically and rationally, in a modernist mode. Where people's positions did not win out they often talked about others being misguided by their selfish, modernist interests that had blinded them to the balanced view. And those who talked more frequently about diverging values – various environmentalists – relied on mainstream, modernist, natural science methods in much of their work.

Reason and technical knowledge seemed as important in Rouse Hill in the 1990s as it was among the high modernist French colonial planners and architects working in the nineteenth and early twentieth centuries and described by Rabinow (1989). Perhaps these forms of knowledge were actually more important in the 1990s as both analytical capacities and the (perception of) problems had increased. While in these times of accelerated and sometimes confusing changes in the wider natural and social environment there was, perhaps, slightly more public disagreement about urban issues than in the recent past, people weren't giving up on truth, rationality, and a clear set of values about better and worse outcomes (Harvey 1996, 2). While the sheer competition of rational and holistic perspectives tended to relegate each one to being just one of many other possible positions, this variety was certainly not limitless (see also Gottdiener 1977, 117; Meyerson and Banfield 1955, 326).

These claims of broader views related to evidence beyond the Rouse Hill site and demonstrated different ways of understanding the public interest. Expansionists and developers claimed to represent the widest set of public preferences and repeatedly quoted surveys showing that most Australians wanted detached houses; accusing opponents of denying the working class their hard-won heritage. In their view individual preference matched the wider public good. Consolidationists and scientific environmentalists had a more indirect or even elitist argument, claiming to represent the long-term common interest in terms of environmental issues and then trying to sell this to the public. These groups, concerned about economic constraints and environmental damage, did tap into larger public debates and concerns about economic security and ecological sustainability, but these debates had not yet transformed housing preferences on the fringe. Even local environmentalists and local speculators argued in terms of a larger set priorities. For local environmentalists stopping growth would preserve what they considered to be a unique locality for the benefit of the rest of Sydney. Local speculators, in contrast, accepted the government's metropolitan planning decisions as representing legitimate public decision making and tried to make the best of it. Although some form of private interest explanation can be used to understand some of the groups' actions this would oversimplify most perspectives.

These claims of breadth and reasonableness perhaps also had a role as a kind of metaphysical consolation. In a context of disagreement – the multiple frameworks – and of change, a sense of certainty, correctness, or truth seemed essential for most sides. In Rouse Hill this certainty came, at least rhetorically or strategically, from superior rationality. In this it echoed Ignatieff's (1984, 62–63) and Brown's (1967, 374) discussions of the Augustinian distinction between two sorts of freedom – the freedom to choose one's beliefs, and the freedom to know one has chosen correctly (see also Augustine 1943 [orig. 399]; MacIntyre 1988, 157; Markus 1967). For Augustine the first was part of basic humanity but the second could only be gained through God's grace. Of course other people have found certainty in the fulfillment of desire, the continuity of tradition, and so on. For the people I interviewed and observed, this freedom of knowing one's beliefs were correct seemed to come through having what they considered to be superior knowlege; rational and balanced ideas about urban form. That gave them a kind of freedom to impose their ideas on the landscape; it made their ideas seem more powerful to themselves. For the moderns I interviewed and observed, Augustine's grace was replaced by trust in knowledge.

Although these ideas of holism, rationality, balance, or seeing the total picture seemed important to most people involved in Rouse Hill, planners were expected by themselves and most others to be the professionals that actually took an overview role in urban development. Balance, holism, and rationality were expected in both their working process and in their substantive vision of urban form. The reality of planners' influence was often much narrower than these expectations, however, with planners only in control of small pieces of the picture, such as land use functions or approvals for individual developments.[2] Planners were expected to be referees in the larger process or perhaps advocates for coordination but had little actual power to do this.

This discussion about public interests, truth, and urban form raises another issues to do with the comparative weakness of arguments about society compared with those about the economy and the natural environment. I was struck by how in debates about human services and social life people could appeal only to a weak "context of broadly shared ideals" about society or social responsibility (Marris 1987, 160). The absence of a strong popular conversation about society, or elite support for funding human services, made those interested in social issues seem like admirable but lonely advocates for a lost cause. Perhaps the high period of urban planning being centrally concerned with creating a better society is over. The natural environment and economy are claiming the center for many of those involved in making and protesting urban developments with people relegated to the role of damagers (for the most idealistic) or consumers (for the others). Perhaps, in this sense, the people I studied were moving beyond a modernist sensibility concerned with human progress, but this movement was not of a character that is clarified being called postmodern.

Change and Responsibility

In Rouse Hill economic and administrative resources were important, particularly the resources to stay in the project for decades and to mandate or fund physical infrastructure. The planning process, a set of legal and administrative activities, formed the context that all groups had to work within, manipulate, or subvert. The Department of Housing and private developer lobby pushed the project through many crises under both Liberal and Labor governments. Community opposition groups seemed to last a few years and then fold. They lacked resources and a certain legitimacy in the planning process that those developing the land were given automatically through their ownership of land, or through the investments they would make providing infrastructure and services.

In New South Wales the state government had a great deal of influence with federal and local governments following along. The state government had the power to stop the development: by not funding it, not allowing private funding, or by imposing restrictions that made it too expensive. The state was also a key player in shaping the character of the development both through the Department of Planning's overview role, and through the design of particular components by departments dealing with areas like housing, transport, education, and health. However, state action met both resistance and constraint. Local governments resisted by seeking to adhere strongly to the formal planning process and the federal government imposed borrowing restrictions and sought to reshape the climate of ideas about urban growth.

Of course this makes it appear that the state government was unified, something even the state Premier Greiner at the time of my fieldwork had to admit was untrue. He put this succinctly in his cover letter for the New South Wales Government's submission to the Industry Commission Inquiry into Taxation and Financial Policy Impacts on Urban Settlement.

> *To purport to provide a single NSW Government submission would not do justice to the many complex issues and perspectives involved.*
> *Accordingly, I am forwarding the submissions made by the various interested government agencies. They contain the views of those agencies and are not necessarily the views of the Government. (NSW 1992c, n.p.)*

The state government's pluralism meant that a more accurate reading of the government's role in Rouse Hill reveals particular departments and even persons having the upper hand at various times, imposing their service standards and funding their projects. In Rouse Hill the shifting relationships of the Department of Planning, the Department of Housing, and the Water Board showed this most clearly.

Given Rouse Hill's lengthy planning process, and the major debates it coincided with, tensions arose between flexibility and continuity, responsiveness to change and holding the urban development and planning process steady enough to give the kind of certainty that enabled action. Expansionists and developers favored

continuity in Rouse Hill's physical form. Environmentalists were
more apocalyptic, warning of impending danger brought on by
old-style development practices. They tried to persuade others of
the necessity of reshaping land development practices.

These issues of change raise additional questions about the character of responsibility in terms of how patterns of underlying responsibilities structured the ways that people faced change. For
private sector developers responsibility was typically toward their
share holders. While state government documents claimed that their
privatization guidelines would ensure full "community" accountability (State Development 1990, 5) this was not quite the case in
Rouse Hill. As a developer explained, the private sector did not
have the same requirements for openness as government, even when
taking over what had previously been a government role.

> *The legal agreements [for the consortium] are based very
> much on a commercial sort of arrangement. And I think
> it's difficult for governments in general to enter into a
> pure commercial arrangement simply because they've
> got, probably not necessarily a greater accountability to
> the public, but certainly a greater perception of account-
> ability. I mean in private organizations directors are
> accountable to shareholders and that sort of thing, but
> for a start you don't have as many shareholders and you
> also, I guess, don't have the same sorts of Freedom of
> Information problems. (Timothy, interview)*

While the public sector developer, the Department of Housing,
was theoretically responsible to a wider public, its practice was far
more like that of a private developer.

Scientific environmentalists saw their responsibility both very
broadly to the wider human and non-human world, but also quite
narrowly in that their perspective was focused on physical survival.
For those in the government this could conflict with their job
descriptions, often tied to a responsibility for particular aspect of
the environment – water, pollution control – and with administrative boundaries that rarely reflected the geography of the natural systems that were of primary concern to this group. This made
this group particularly susceptible to leaking documents (if in the

bureaucracy) and to using the media in ways that would expand the debate.

Expansionists, rather than focusing on the natural environment, thought in terms of their responsibilities within a social world structured in terms of class and family type. They were oriented toward nuclear families, and the middle and working classes. Consolidationists, in contrast, shared the environmental concerns of the scientific environmentalists but saw the human groups to whom they were responsible as a diverse array of household types with changing needs. However, both consolidationists' and expansionists' jobs primarily involved responsibility for zoning and development approval and thus their wider social concerns had to be served through manipulating physical space. Local environmentalists and other locals, pragmatically, focused on their own land and themselves although within the context of a wider debate about the place of individuals (adversely) affected by metropolitan planning.

As a spatial, social, and temporal activity, urban planning was made more complex by these different understandings of, and constraints on, responsibilities. Agreeing on the character of the important spatial areas, human and non-human groups, and important time frames, presupposed a level of common understandings about what was important and reflected a set of power relations. Airsheds, local government areas, families, and 20 years into the future, were all possible limits on responsibilities – singularly and in concert – but all open to contest. Could environmentalists impose their definitions of regions based on air movement where the traditional boundaries were of metropolitan or local government areas? Which human groups counted as families: the "nuclear" groupings of the expansionists or the small households talked about by consolidationists? Was 20 years irrelevantly long or impossibly shortsighted? Perhaps, for example, airsheds were the trendy concerns of the 1990s to be reduced in significance when technological innovations eliminated air pollution. Local government areas, in contrast, could become the future vital centers of democratic participation.

While groups like local environmentalists often called for long-term planning, this may have been more of a problem than a benefit to them as it tended to lock in a set of ideas that became outdated in their terms. The balanced, broad, or rational view of one period could seem hopelessly narrow and irrational in another where a different kind of public was making judgments about quality of life.

As the development stretched across decades, individuals were concerned with, and responsible for, different components – spatially and substantively – in different periods. In this context of multiple players, multiple actions, and multiple concerns, a sense of personal responsibility – even in a narrow area of professional interest or one's job description – was hard to maintain. Who was responsible for Rouse Hill? Can there be guilt or pride about such a diffuse and ambiguous project?

This is a complex question. Rouse Hill is the result of a lengthy, multi-stage, formal planning process, already stretching through three decades and involving metropolitan, regional, and local planning as well as coordination through interdepartmental committees. Cabinet members or the executives of the consortium had a high level of power to approve and fund development; middle-level professionals giving advice within the context of their professional expertise shaped only some of the options available.

Planners seemed to resolve this tension by articulating goals that were far more general than their scope of influence. Plans often contained a wider set of aims – in the discussion sections – than the legal instruments actually enforced. That a guiding principle could not be realized practically became a recurring theme in the development of Rouse Hill. In principle the Rouse Hill Infrastructure Consortium reduced Water Board financial commitments to "virtually zero" (Timothy, interview). In practice this was not so certain as "these figures will be influenced by the rate of development demand in the Rouse Hill Development Area" (Nedeljkovic 1991, 10). Human services were classed as "basic" services in the draft Regional Environmental Plan (DEP 1986b, 15), but in practice funding these services was an acute problem that no one had solved in years of detailed planning. In principle Rouse Hill was to provide housing for first-home buyers; however, this became increasingly difficult as infrastructure costs rose.

In each case the goals were not, even could not be, implemented. Their presence, however, said something about the concerns of the writers, or about the way that they wanted to be seen by others. They provided a history of hopes that future bureaucrats could call upon as evidence of original intentions, embedding fairly narrow mandates in a larger context. They made the plans seem generous and comprehensive, in contrast to their far narrower enforceable sections. In a fundamental way they represented the public's interests and concerns, although interests and concerns could not be stated or carried out in a coherent way. However, they were misleading in that the legal requirements not only did far less than the planning goals promised, but quite often did something quite different. The Water Board's financial commitment was not virtually eliminated; human services were not adequately funded.

What then does this mean about the role and meaning of planning in times of change? I have several concluding thoughts. For planners and for others something like a public interest is still important, but its character is interpreted very differently by different groups. In Rouse Hill there was both more certainty and more incoherence about the concept that I had expected to find even within individual work units. Given the divided ideas and interests among various parts of government, and the relative flexibility of developers to embrace different urban forms and planning processes, the power of capital or of the state is not inevitably tied to one approach to urban development.

In a long running project such as this one, that is set in a complex and changing context, several generations' ideas about the best form of urban development had managed to shape the process. Economic issues such as providing housing for workers and supplying housing demand remained important throughout the planning process. Although in the earlier periods of the development a significant group of planners was concerned with social issues this was increasingly overshadowed by a sense of urgency about protecting the natural world. Concerns about nature and about social goals such as equality and opportunity are not necessarily incompatible, of course, as the consolidationists argued. However, for many people this concern with the natural environment was a major shift in thinking. It is a shift that is likely to frame debates about urban growth for a significant period.

End Notes

[1]   This echoes Marris' analysis of community development projects in Britain (Marris 1987, 50).

[2]   Stronger coordinating roles seem to be coming into being increasingly through environmental bureaucracies and legislation, or through privatization shifting coordination and development functions to the private sector. Thus someone will have this kind of strong coordinating role in the future. However, those performing these roles will likely be environmental policy makers or developers, less interested than city planners in the social assumptions and implications of their ideas and actions.

Abbreviations

ASC	Australian Securities Commission
CEPA	(Australian) Commonwealth Environmental Protection Agency
CHANGE	Coalition of Hawkesbury and Nepean Groups for the Environment
CSIRO	(Australian) Commonwealth Scientific Investigation and Research Organisation
DCP	Development Control Plan
DCS	(New South Wales) Department of Community Services
DEP	(New South Wales) Department of Environment and Planning (1980 to 1988)
DHHCS	(Australian) Department of Health, Housing and Community Services
DoH	(New South Wales) Department of Housing, prior to 1986 Housing Commission and Land Commission
DoP	(New South Wales) Department of Planning (1988 to 1995), formerly Department of Environment and Planning (1980 to 1988), Planning and Environment Commission (1974 to 1980), and State Planning Authority (1963 to 1974). From 1995 onwards the Department of Urban Affairs and Planning.
EP&A Act	(New South Wales) Environmental Planning and Assessment Act (1979)
EIS	Environmental Impact Statement
HCC	(New South Wales) Housing Committee of Cabinet
HIA	Housing Industry Association
LEP	Local Environmental Plan
MWS&DB	Metropolitan Water Sewerage and Drainage Board, now simply the Water Board
NHS	National Housing Strategy
NSW	New South Wales
REP	Regional Environmental Plan
RES	Regional Environmental Study
RHCPT	Rouse Hill Community Planning Team
RHDA	Rouse Hill Development Area
RHIC	Rouse Hill Infrastructure Consortium
RTA	(New South Wales) Roads and Traffic Authority

SEPP	State Environmental Planning Policy
SPA	(New South Wales) State Planning Authority (1963 to 1974)
SPCC	(New South Wales) State Pollution Control Commission
SROP	Sydney Region Outline Plan
UDC	(New South Wales) Urban Development Committee
UDP	(New South Wales) Urban Development Program
WSROC	Western Sydney Regional Organisation of Councils

CHRONOLOGY

1948   Cumberland Plan published by Cumberland County Council: Rouse Hill located outside urban area.

1951   Gazettal (official acceptance) of Cumberland Plan.

1963   New South Wales State Planning Authority (SPA) formed as the state planning agency.

1968   Sydney Regional Outline Plan, the new metropolitan plan, published by SPA. North West Sector, including Rouse Hill, indicated for future investigation for urban development.

1974   State Planning Authority is transformed into Planning and Environment Commission.

1976   Labor elected in New South Wales (NSW) replacing long-term Liberal government.

c.1980 State planning agency buys Mungarie Park golf course for North West Sector regional center.

1980   Planning and Environment Commission is transformed into Department of Environment and Planning (DEP).

1980   June: Review of Sydney Regional Outline Plan published by DEP.

1980   September: Urban Development Committee established following review of Sydney Region Outline Plan "to provide a co-ordinated forum to advise the Government through the Minister of Planning and Environment on all matters of urban development," enabling a more orderly process of supplying residential land (DEP 1984a, 9). Membership was from several different agencies.

1980   December: Consultant report by Patrick Troy recommends preparing an outline plan for the North West Sector and Development Coordinating Committee of state cabinet requests structure plans of North West Sector.

1982   January: Structure Plan presented to Urban Development Committee of state cabinet.

1982   May: Structure Plan presented to Housing Committee of Cabinet (HCC). HCC requests new Urban Development Committee report on order of priority of four areas, including two locations in the North West Sector.

1983   March: Medium Term Options Study presented to Housing Committee of Cabinet. Used planning balance sheet style cost–benefit analysis to select Rouse Hill in North West Sector as most suitable medium term development option, for production by 1990.

1983   April: Urban Development Committee establishes North West Sector Subcommittee.

1984   July: North West Sector Regional Environmental Study, undertaken by Department of Environment and Planning, released for public comment. On exhibition 30 July to 28 September. Start of public planning process.

1986   October: Rouse Hill Development Area North West Sector Draft Regional Environmental Plan released for public comment. On exhibition October 1986 to May 1987: 250 submissions received.

1988   Department of Environment and Planning is transformed into Department of Planning (DoP).

1988   February: Metropolitan Strategy published by DoP.

1988   March: Liberal–National Party government elected in New South Wales after 12 years of Labor.

1988   September: First meeting of interdepartmental Human Services Working Party/Group for the Rouse Hill Development Area, reporting ultimately to the Urban Development Committee.

1988   Late in year: Proposal for infrastructure privatization through Rouse Hill Infrastructure Consortium (RHIC) put to NSW State cabinet.

1989   February: Registration of Rouse Hill Infrastructure Consortium.

1989   February: Department of Planning establishes Joint Release Area Management Committee to oversee release of Stage One of Rouse Hill Development Area.

1989   Mid-year: Rouse Hill Infrastructure Consortium proposal initially accepted by NSW government.

1989   September: Publication of Rouse Hill Development Area Regional Environmental Plan by the DoP.

1989   September: Seminar held by Department of Planning for non-government human service agencies leads to formation of Rouse Hill Community Planning Team, a coalition of such groups.

1990 May: Deed (agreement) between Rouse Hill Infrastructure Consortium and Water Board signed.

1990 June: Draft Local Environmental Plan for Parklea Release Area in the Rouse Hill Development Area placed on exhibition by Blacktown City Council for 17 weeks from 13 June: 73 submissions from private sector, 52 public authorities consulted with.

1990 June: Bob Wilson, Managing Director of Water Board, makes speech to Urban Development Institute of Australia questioning whether urban development should continue in western Sydney, the site of Rouse Hill.

1990 June: Draft Local Environmental Plan for Kellyville-Rouse Hill placed on exhibition by Baulkham Hills Shire Council from 12 June to 30 October. Almost 1000 written submissions received, mostly dealing with road works and zoning in particular locations.

1990 November: Three days of public hearings on Blacktown Local Environmental Plan by Commissioner William Simpson.

1990 December: Completion of final "Pilot Study" on air quality in Macarthur South and South Creek Valley, two major growth corridors to the south-west of Sydney. Report by Hyde and Johnson not released until 1991.

1991 January: Environmental Impact Statement for Proposed Rouse Hill Sewerage Treatment Plant, written by Manidis Roberts Consultants, placed on exhibition January to March: 48 submissions received in comment.

1991 Early in year: Local Environmental Plan for Parklea Release Area in Blacktown made official.

1991 May: Three day smog "event" in Sydney with severe brown haze.

1991 June: Determining authority's report (acceptance) of Environmental Impact Statement for Rouse Hill Sewage Treatment Plant published. Water Board is determining authority.

1991 June: Local Environmental Plan for Kellyville/Rouse Hill Release Area in Baulkham Hills made official.

1991 July: Air Quality "Smog" Summit held by state government.

1991 July: Due to mismanagement, Baulkham Hills Shire

Council has general manager appointed stripping it of financial and management powers.

1991   October: Terry Metherell resigns from Liberal Party to join four other independents in state parliament. Liberal–National Party government now hold only 48 seats out of 99 in lower house. Cites poor planning of North West Sector as one reason for resignation.

1991   November: Public meeting with 120 in attendance calls for halt to Rouse Hill.

1992   February: Second Smog Summit.

1992   July: New state government cabinet announced after resignation of Premier Greiner. Minister for Planning given Ministry of Housing as added responsibility.

1993   Discussion paper published by DoP setting out proposals for changing the 1988 metropolitan plan.

1993–   Development Control Plans released for first areas in both
1994   Baulkham Hills and Blacktown.

1994   First lots produced in Rouse Hill Development Area.

1995   DoP release the new metropolitan plan, "Cities for the 21st Century." Rouse Hill development scaled back.

1995   Labor replaces Liberal–National Party coalition in New South Wales government.

1995   Department of Planning is transformed into Department of Urban Affairs and Planning.

1996   Liberal–National Party government replaces Labor at federal level.

References

Adams, Carolyn, 1991. Urban regions as educational laboratories. *Metropolitan Universities* 2, 2: 37–46.

Adams, Paul, 1992. Television as gathering place. *Annals of the Association of American Geographers* 82: 117–135.

Aldridge, Meryl, 1979. *The British new towns: A programme without a policy.* London: Routledge and Kegan Paul.

Allison, Col, 1991a. Smog hit councils want quick action. *Sydney Morning Herald*, 22 May, 4.

—, 1991b. No Waste Plan for Cities Says Doctor. *Sydney Morning Herald*, 4 December, 6.

Altshuler, Alan, 1965. *The city planning process: A political analysis.* Ithaca, New York: Cornell University Press.

Appadurai, Arjun, 1974. Right and left hand castes in South India. *Indian Economic and Social History Review* 11, 2–3: 216–259.

Appleyard, Donald, 1976. *Planning a pluralist city: Conflicting realities in Ciudad Guyana.* Cambridge, Massachusetts: MIT Press.

Augustine, 1943 (orig. 399). *The confessions.* Translated by F. J. Sheed. New York: Sheed and Ward.

Australian Securities Commission, 1992. Company extracts from Australian Securities Commission computer database.

—, 1993. Company extracts from Australian Securities Commission computer database.

Bailey, Paul, 1991. The west is sick of Sydney's bad air. *Sydney Morning Herald*, 1 July, 5.

Banerjee, Tridib, and William Baer, 1984. *Beyond the neighborhood unit: Residential environments and public policy.* New York: Plenum Press.

Barthes, Roland, 1980. *New critical essays.* Translated by Richard Howard. New York: Hill and Wang.

Barry, Brian, 1965. *Political argument.* New York: Humanities Press.

Baulkham Hills Shire Council, 1990. *Kellyville-Rouse Hill draft local environmental plan: Planning and urban investigation report.* Sydney: Baulkham Hills Shire Council.

—, 1991. *Rouse Hill draft local environmental plan: Submission pursuant to section 68 of the EP and A Act 1979 and supplementary information.* Sydney: Baulkham Hills Shire Council.

168 CONSTRUCTING SUBURBS

Baulkham Hills Council Environmental Services Division, 1993. *Kellyville/Rouse Hill landscape and urban design strategy: Draft framework.* Baulkham Hills: Baulkham Hills Council.

—, 1994a. *Development control plan: Rouse Hill neighborhood.* Baulkham Hills: Baulkham Hills Council.

—, 1994b. *Kellyville/Rouse Hill residential development control plan.* Baulkham Hills: Baulkham Hills Council.

Baum, Howell, 1983. *Planners and public expectations.* Cambridge, Massachusetts: Schenkman.

Beauregard, Robert, 1993. *Voices of decline: The postwar fate of US cities.* Cambridge, Massachusetts: Blackwell.

Beder, Sharon, 1989. *Toxic fish and sewer surfing: How deceit and collusion are destroying our great beaches.* Sydney: Allen and Unwin.

Bellah, Robert, Richard Madsen, William Sullivan, Ann Swindler, and Stephen Tipton, 1985. *Habits of the heart: Individualism and commitment in American life.* Berkeley: University of California Press.

Berkhout Planning and Development Consultants, 1992. *Parklea urban release area: Development concepts for the Department of Housing land in the Glenwood Precinct.* Report prepared in conjunction with Woodhead Australia for the NSW Department of Housing. Sydney: Berkhout Planning and Develpment Consultants.

Berman, Marshall, 1988. *All that is solid melts into air: The experience of modernity.* New York: Penguin.

Bernstein, Richard, 1976. *The restructuring of social and political theory.* New York: Harcourt Brace Jovanovich.

Bird, Neil, 1991a. A developer's perspective in supply of residential land: Fluctuations in the housing industry and the IPC report. *Australian Planner* 21, 1: 22–23.

—, 1991b. Housing and population: The development industry response. In *Western Sydney's growth can we manage it? Papers, summary of workshops and future strategies.* Blacktown: Western Sydney Regional Organisation of Councils.

Blacktown City Council, 1984. *Review of the regional environmental study for the North West Sector.* Chief Town Planner's report number 1264(D). Sydney: Blacktown City Council.

—, 1987. *Review of the draft regional environmental plan for the Rouse Hill Development Area.* Chief Town Planner's report number 1923(D). Blacktown City Council.

—, c1990. *Parklea release area: Draft local environmental plan explanatory material.* Blacktown: Blacktown City Council.

—, 1991. *Parklea release area: Adoption of local environmental plan.* Town Planning Report Number 194(N). Blacktown: Blacktown City Council.

Boson, Mary, 1989. The new mini-city is a tall order. *Northern Herald, Sydney Morning Herald,* 16 March, 4–5.

Boyer, Christine, 1983. *Dreaming the rational city.* Cambridge, Massachusetts: MIT Press.

Boylen, Louise, 1991. City people moving to urban fringes. *Australian Financial Review*, 12 June, 7.

Brindle, Ray, 1992. Toronto – Paradigm lost? *Australian Planner* 30, 3: 123–30.

Brown, Peter, 1967. *Augustine of Hippo*. Berkeley: University of California Press.

Bruner, Edward, 1986. Ethnography as narrative. In *The anthropology of experience*. Edited by Victor Turner and Edward Bruner. Urbana: University of Illinois Press.

Bruntland Commission, 1987. *Our common future*. United Nations Commission on Environment and Development. Oxford: Oxford University Press.

Burby, Raymond, Shirley Weiss, and Robert Zehner, 1975. National evaluation of community services and quality of life in American new towns. *Public Administration Review* 35, 3: 229–239.

Burgess, Catriona. No date. *The Nepean Hawkesbury: A river running out of time*. Sydney: Water Board.

Calavita, Nico, and Roger Caves, 1994. Planners' attitudes toward growth; A comparative case study. *Journal of the American Planning Association* 60, 4: 483–500.

Camp Scott Furphy, c. 1984. *Report on nutrient removal at Riverstone and Rouse Hill W.P.C.P.S*. Sydney: Metropolitan Water Sewerage and Drainage Board.

Camp Scott Furphy, and Hawkesbury Agricultural College, 1988. *Urban runoff study*. Windsor: Joint Councils River Committee.

Cardew, Richard, 1985. Have we been operating under the wrong paradigm? A reinterpretation of urban residential property markets. In *Living in cities: Urbanism and society in metropolitan Australia*. Edited by Ian Burnley and James Forrest. Sydney: Allen and Unwin with the Geographical Society of New South Wales.

—, 1988. *Land market supply relationships*. A report prepared for the NSW Department of Housing. Sydney: Centre for Environmental and Urban Studies, Macquarie University.

—, 1997. Personal communication, 6 February.

Castles, Ian, 1988. *Census 86, Australia in profile: A summary of major findings*. Canberra: Australian Bureau of Statistics.

—, 1994. *Yearbook Australia 1994*. Canberra: Australian Bureau of Statistics.

Cervero, Robert, 1989. *America's suburban centers: The land use-transportation link*. Boston: Unwin-Hyman.

—, 1990. Congestion relief; The land use alternative. *Journal of Planning Education and Research* 10, 2: 119–129.

Cities Commission (of Australia), 1975. *New structures for Australian cities*. Main report. Prepared by Maunsell and Partners. No place of publication.

Clark, S.D. 1966. *The suburban society*. Toronto: University of Toronto Press.

Clarke, Harry, Anthony Chisholm, Geoff Edwards, and John Kennedy, 1990. *Immigration, population growth and the environment*. Canberra: Australian Governement Publishing Service.

Clavel, Pierre, 1983. *Opposition planning in Wales and Appalachia*. Philadelphia: Temple University Press.

Clifford, James, 1988a. *The predicament of culture*. Cambridge, Massachusetts: Harvard University Press.

—, 1988b. Identity in Mashpee. In *The predicament of culture*. Cambridge, Massachusetts: Harvard University Press.

Collins, Jock, 1988. *Migrant hands in a distant land: Australia's post-war immigration*. Sydney: Pluto Press.

Committee to Advise on Australia's Immigration Policies, 1988. *Immigration: A commitment to Australia*. Canberra: Australian Government Publishing Service.

Commonwealth Environmental Protection Agency, 1992. *Urban consolidation: An environment perspective*. Conference proceedings. Canberra: Australian Government Publishing Service.

Connell, R.W. 1990. The state, gender and sexual politics: Theory and appraisal. *Theory and Society* 19, 5: 507–544.

Cook, Danielle, 1991a. Problems council given a reprieve. *Sydney Morning Herald*, 3 August.

—, 1991b. Mayors march in planning protest. *Sydney Morning Herald*, 3 December, 6.

Cooper, Dave,1994. Portraits of paradise: Themes and images of the tourist industry. *Southeast Asian Journal of Social Science* 22, 1: 144–160.

Cosgrove, Denis, 1984. *Social formation and symbolic landscape*. London: Croom Helm.

Coultan, Mark, 1992. New blood does little to exorcise Greiner's ghost. *Sydney Morning Herald*, 3 July, 4.

Cumberland County Council, 1948. *The planning scheme for the County of Cumberland, New South Wales*. Sydney: Cumberland County Council.

Dalton, Barbara, 1980. *Problems faced by residents of new communities*. Report for the Sydney Western Sub-Region Planning Team. Sydney: Planning and Environment Commission.

Dalton, Linda, 1989. Emerging knowledge about planning practice. *Journal of Planning Education and Research* 9, 1: 29–44.

Daly, Maurice, 1982. *Sydney boom, Sydney bust: The city and its property market 1850–1981*. Sydney: George Allen and Unwin.

Dear, Michael, 1989. Survey 16: Privatization and the rhetoric of planning practice. *Environment and Planning D* 7, 4: 449–462.

Department of Community Services, 1992. In submission by New South Wales Government to inquiry on taxation and financial policy impacts on urban settlements. Canberra: Industry Commission.

Department of Environment and Planning, 1980. *Review of the Sydney region outline plan*. Sydney: Department of Environment and Planning.

—, 1982. *North West Sector: Structure plan*. Sydney: Department of Environment and Planning.

—, 1983. Medium term options for the Sydney region. Report to the Housing Commission of Cabinet by Urban Development Committee. Copy in author's files.

—, 1984a. *Sydney region North West Sector: Regional environmental study*. Two Volumes and Summary. Sydney: Department of Environment and Planning.

—, 1984b. Report to Housing Committee [of Cabinet] on North West Sector. Annexure to Urban Development Committee Report Number 26/84, File Number 84/10048. Sydney: Department of Environment and Planning.

—, 1986a. *Draft Sydney regional environmental plan, Rouse Hill Development Area, North West Sector.* Sydney: Department of Environment and Planning.

—, 1986b. *Draft Sydney regional environmental plan, Rouse Hill Development Area, North West Sector: Supporting information.* Sydney: Department of Environment and Planning.

Department of Family and Community Services, 1990. *Rouse Hill Development Area Service Plan.* Sydney: Department of Family and Community Services.

Department of Health, Housing and Community Services, 1992a. *Housing-choices for a changing nation: Budget 1992–93.* Canberra: Australian Government Publishing Service.

—, 1992b. *Indicative Planning Council for the Housing Industry: Residential land report, 1992.* Canberra: Australian Government Publishing Service.

—, 1992c. *Better cities: National developments 1991–1992.* Canberra: Australian Government Publishing Service.

Department of Housing, 1989. *Annual report.* Sydney: Department of Housing.

—, 1990. *Annual report.* Sydney: Department of Housing.

—, 1991. *Annual report.* Sydney: Department of Housing.

—, 1997. World wide web page. New South Wales Government Information Service. http://203.102.130.82/cgi-bin/genobject/Housing/section_5/tigqm V97bC. Correct as of July.

Department of Industry, Technology and Commerce, 1990. *Indicative Planning Council for the Housing Industry: Residential land report 1990.* Canberra: Australian Government Publishing Service.

—, 1991. *Indicative Planning Council for the Housing Industry: Residential land report 1991.* Canberra: Australian Government Publishing Service.

Department of Planning, 1988. *Sydney into its third century: Metropolitan strategy for the Sydney region.* Sydney: Department of Planning.

—, 1989a. *Rouse Hill Development Area: Sydney regional environmental plan number 19.* Sydney: Department of Planning.

—, 1989b. *Hawkesbury-Nepean River: Sydney regional environmental plan number 20.* Sydney: Department of Planning.

—, 1990. *Guidelines for levying section 94 contributions: Discussion paper.* Sydney: Department of Planning.

—, 1991a. *South Creek Valley, south western Sydney: Regional environmental study.* Sydney: Department of Planning.

—, 1991b. *South Creek Valley, south western Sydney: Draft Sydney regional environmental plan.* Sydney: Department of Planning.

—, 1991c. *Macarthur South: Regional environmental study.* Sydney: Department of Planning.

—, 1991d. *Urban consolidation (redevelopment of urban land): State environmental planning policy number 32.* Sydney: Department of Planning.

—, 1991e. *Dual occupancy subdivision in urban areas: State environmental planning policy 25, amendment number two.* Sydney: Department of Planning.

—, 1992. *Updating the metropolitan strategy: Invitation for comment.* Sydney: Department of Planning.

—, 1993. *Sydney's future.* Sydney: Department of Planning.

—, 1995. *Cities for the 21st century.* Sydney: Department of Planning.

Department of Transport, 1992. In submission by New South Wales Government to inquiry on taxation and financial policy impacts on urban settlements. Canberra: Industry Commission.

Development Corporation of New South Wales, 1969. *Report on selective decentralization: The case for concentration upon growth points as a strategy for effective decentralization.* Sydney: Development Corporation.

Dodds, Alan, 1991. Water quality in the Hawkesbury-Nepean River system. In *Western Sydney's growth can we manage it? Papers, summary of workshops and future strategies.* Blacktown: Western Sydney Regional Organisation of Councils.

Dorst, John, 1989. *The written suburb: An American site, an ethnographic dilemma.* Philadelphia: University of Pennsylvania Press.

Douglas, Jack, 1976. *Investigative social research: Individual and team field research.* Beverly Hills, California: sage.

Dubbink, David, 1984. I'll have my town medium-rural, please. *Journal of the American Planning Association* 50, 4: 406–418.

Earthworm, 1991. Special on transport planning presented by Rebecca Latham and produced by Carolyn Wenzel. Australian Broadcasting Corporation, Radio National.

Edwards, Meredith, 1991. *The national housing strategy: Framework for reform.* National Housing Strategy background paper number 1. Canberra: Australian Government Publishing Service.

Engel, David, 1984. The oven bird's song: Insiders, outsiders, and personal injuries in an American community. *Law and Society Review* 18, 4: 552–582.

Entrekin, Nicholas, 1991. *The betweenness of place: Toward a geography of modernity.* Houndmills, Hampshire: MacMillan.

Evans, David, 1988. Social interaction and conflict over residential growth: A structuration perspective. In *Qualitative methods in human geography.* Edited by John Eyeles and David Smith. Cambridge, United Kingdom: Polity Press.

Evill, B.1995. Population, urban density, and fuel use: Eliminating spurious correlation. *Urban Policy and Research* 13, 1: 29–36.

Ewing, Reid, 1997. Is Los Angeles-style sprawl desirable? *Journal of the American Planning Association* 63, 1: 107–126.

Fagan, Bob, 1986. Industrial restructuring and the metropolitan fringe: Growth and disadvantage in western Sydney. *Australian Planner* 24, 1: 11–17.

Fainstein, Susan, 1994. *The city builders: Property, politics and planning in London and New York.* Cambridge, Massachusetts: Blackwell.

Farr, Malcolm, 1991. City Squeeze plan "cheaper". *Telegraph Mirror* early edition, 21 August, 8.

Feizkhah, Elizabeth, 1994. *Rouse Hill infrastructure project.* Sydney: Rouse Hill Infrastructure Consortium (Mile End Road, Rouse Hill, NSW 2155).

Feld, Marcia, and John Hohman, 1989. Planning leadership: A tale of two cities. *Journal of the American Planning Association* 55, 4: 479–481.

Fincher, Ruth, 1991. *Immigration, urban infrastructure and the environment.* Canberra: Australian Government Publishing Service.

Finlay, Alan, 1994. We're not on the road to LA. *Sydney Morning Herald* 30 June, 9.

Forester, John, 1989. *Planning in the face of power.* Berkeley: University of California Press.

—, 1992. *On the ethics of planning: Profiles of planners and what they teach us about practical judgment and moral improvisation.* Cornell University working papers in planning number 117. Ithaca, New York: Cornell University Department of City Regional Planning.

—, 1993. *Learning from practice stories and the priority of practical of judgment.* Cornell University working papers in planning number 130, Ithaca, New York: Cornell University Department of City and Regional Planning.

Forsyth, Ann, 1995. Privatization: Infrastructure on the urban edge. *Journal of Urban Affairs* 17, 3: 241–262.

—, 1997. Five images of a suburb: Perspectives on a new urban development. *Journal of the American Planning Association* 63, 1: 45–60.

—, Forthcoming 1998. Soundbite cities: Imagining futures in debates over urban form. *Journal of Architectural and Planning Research.*

Foucault, Michel, 1980. *Power/knowledge: Selected interviews and other writings 1972–1977.* Edited by Colin Gordon. New York: Pantheon.

Frank, James, 1989. *The costs of alternative development patterns: A review of the literature.* Washington, DC: Urban Land Institute.

Freestone, Robert, 1992. Sydney's green belt 1945–1960. *Australian Planner* 30, 2: 70–77.

Frieden, Bernard, and Lynne Sagalyn, 1989. *Downtown, Inc.: How America rebuilds cities.* Cambridge, Massachusetts: MIT Press.

Friedmann, John, 1987. *Planning in the public domain: From knowledge to action.* Princeton: Princeton University Press.

Fulop, Liz, and Dick Sheppard, 1988. The life and death of regional initiatives in western Sydney: The case of the local government development program. *International Journal of Urban and Regional Research* 12, 4: 609–626.

Gans, Herbert, 1967. *The Levittowners: Ways of life and politics in a new suburban community.* New York: Pantheon.

Geertz, Clifford, 1973. *The interpretation of cultures.* New York: Basic Books.

Giddens, Anthony, 1979. *Central problems in social theory.* Berkeley: University of California Press.

Gilligan, Carol, 1982. *In a different voice: Psychological theory and women's development.* Cambridge, Massachusetts: Harvard University Press.

Gilligan, Carol, Janie Ward, and Jill Taylor eds, 1988. *Mapping the moral domain: A contribution of women's thinking to psychological theory and education.* Cambridge, Massachusetts: Center for the Study of Gender, Education and Human Development, Harvard University.

Ginsburg, Faye, 1989. *Contested lives: The abortion debate in an American community.* Berkeley: University of California Press.

Glaser, Barney, and Anselm Strauss, 1967. *The discovery of grounded theory: Strategies for qualitative research.* New York: Aldine de Gruyler.

Gordon, Peter, and H.L. Wong, 1985. The costs of urban sprawl: Some new evidence. *Environmental and Planning* A 17: 661–666.

Gordon, Peter, and Harry Richardson, 1989. Gasoline consumption and cities: A reply. *Journal of the American Planning Association* 55, 3: 342–346.

—, 1997. Where's the sprawl? *Journal of the American Planning Association* 63, 2: 275–278.

Goring, James, 1988. The fictive sense of place: Los Angeles in word and image. *Places* 5, 2: 64–71.

Goss, J., 1993. Placing the market and marketing place: Tourist advertising of the Hawaiian islands, 1972–92. *Environment and Planning D* 11: 663–688.

Gottdiener, Mark, 1977. *Planned sprawl: Private and public interests in suburbia.* Beverly Hills, California: Sage.

—, 1995. *Postmodern semiotics: Material culture and the forms of postmodern life.* Oxford: Blackwell.

Grant, Jill, 1994. *The drama of democracy: Contention and dispute in community planning.* Toronto: University of Toronto Press.

Green, H.R., 1988. Letter to Pat Smith on Department of Planning, Sydney Region West Office letterhead, August 18. Copy in author's files.

Green, Richard, and Robert Zinke, 1993. The rhetorical way of knowing and public administration. *Administration and Society* 25, 3: 317–334.

Greenhiouse, Carol, 1985. Anthropology at home: Whose home? *Human Organization* 44: 261–264.

Gregory, Robert, 1991. How much are Australia's economy and economic policy influenced by the world economy? *In Australia compared: People, policies and politics.* Edited by Francis Castles. North Sydney: Allen and Unwin.

Gyles, R.V., 1992. *Royal Commission into productivity in the building industry in New South Wales.* Final report. Available through the NSW Government Information Services, Sydney.

Hammond, Phillip, Larry Adams, Albert Bergesen, Benton Johnson, Thomas Schrock, and Robert Wuthnow, 1981. The shifting meaning of a wall of separation: Some notes on church, state, and conscience. *Sociological Analysis* 42, 3: 227–234.

Handy, Susan, 1992. *How land use patterns affect travel patterns: A bibiliography.* Bibliography number 279. Chicago: Council of Planning Librarians.

Harley, J.B., 1988. Maps, knowledge and power. In *The iconography of landscape: Essays on the symbolic representation, design, and use of past environments.* Edited by Denis Cosgrove and Stephen Daniels. Cambridge: Cambridge University Press.

Harper, Thomas, and Stanley Stein, 1995. Out of the postmodern abyss: Preserving the rationale for liberal planning. *Journal of Planning Education and Research* 14, 4: 233–244.

Harrison, Peter, 1971. Planning Sydney: Twenty-five years on. *Royal Australian Planning Institute Journal* 9, 4: 122–129.

Harvey, David, 1996. *Justice, nature and the geography of difference.* Cambridge, Massachusetts: Blackwell.

Hendler, Sue, 1991. Ethics in Planning: The views of students and practitioners. *Journal of Planning Education and Research* 10, 2: 99–105.

— ed. 1995. *Planning ethics: A reader in planning theory, practice and education*. New Brunswick, New Jersey: Rutgers Center for Urban Policy Research.

Hertzog Thomas, Stephen Kaplan, and Rachel Kaplan, 1976. The prediction of preference for familiar urban places. *Environment and Behaviour* 8, 4: 627–645.

Hillier, Jean, 1993. To boldly go where no planners have ever. *Environment and Planning D* 11: 89–113.

Hills Mercury, 1991. Public protest at sector plans. 26 November, 10.

Hirst Consulting Services, Conybeare Morrison and Partners, Rankine and Hill, and Project Planning Associates, 1989. *Rouse Hill Development Area: Subregional and district centres planning strategies*. Report number two for NSW Department of Planning. Sydney: Hirst Consulting Services.

Housing Industry Association National Homebuilders Council, 1990. *Housing towards 2000*. Canberra: Housing Industry Association.

Housing Industry Association, 1992. Submission to Industry Commission inquiry on taxation and financial policy impacts on urban settlements. Canberra: Industry Commission.

Howard Tanner and Associates, 1984. *Heritage study of the North Western Sector of Sydney*. Survey for the NSW Department of Environment and Planning. McMahon's Point: Howard Tanner and Associates.

Howe, Brian, 1991. Building better cities: A commonwealth-state partnership. Address to the joint meeting of the Australian Institute of Urban Studies and the Planning Research Centre, University of Sydney, September 17, Photocopy.

Howe, Elizabeth, 1992. Professional roles and the public interest in planning. *Journal of Planning Literature* 6, 3: 230–248.

—, 1994. *Acting on ethics in city planning*. New Brunswick: Center for Urban Policy Research.

Howe, Elizabeth, and Jerome Kaufman, 1979. The ethics of contemporary American planners. *Journal of the American Planning Association* 45, 3: 243–255.

—, 1981. The values of contemporary American planners. *Journal of the American Planning Association* 47, 3: 266-278.

Hughes Trueman Ludlow and Dwyer Leslie, 1991. *Public sector cost savings of urban consolidation*. Final report. Prepared for the NSW Department of Planning, Sydney Water Board and [Australian] Department of Industry, Technology and Commerce. Sydney: Department of Planning.

Hughes, David, 1991. Western Sydney perspective on urban transport options. *On Track: Journal of the Coalition of Transport Action Groups* 3: 7.

Hummon, David, 1986. Urban views: Popular perspectives on city life. *Urban Life* 15, 1: 3–36.

Hyde, Robert and Graham Johnson, 1990. *Pilot study: Evaluation of air quality issues for the development of Macarthur South and the South Creek Valley regions of Sydney*. CSIRO MRL restricted investigation report 1885R. Second printing of final report prepared for the NSW Department of Planning, NSW State Pollution Control Commission, and Commonwealth Department of Transport and Communications, Domestic Aviation Division. Sydney: Department of Planning.

Ignatieff, Michael, 1984. *The needs of strangers*. New York: Penguin.

Innes, Judith, 1996. Planning through consensus building: A new view of the comprehensive planning ideal. *Journal of the American Planning Association* 62, 4: 460–472.

Jack, Rand, and Dana Crowley Jack, 1989. *Moral visions and professional decisions: The changing values of women and men lawyers*. Cambridge: Cambridge Unversity Press.

Johnson, Graham, 1991. Air pollution in Western Sydney. In *Western Sydney's growth can we manage it? Papers, summary of workshops future strategies*. Blacktown: Western Sydney Regional Organisation of Councils.

Johnson, R.J., Derek Gregory, and David Smith, 1994. *The dictionary of human geography*. Third edition. Oxford: Blackwell.

Keating, Paul, 1991. Housing choice and the future of the Australian city. Address to the Public Policy Seminar, Australian National University, Canberra, July 10. Photocopy.

Kenworthy, Jeff, 1991a. The land use and transit connection in Toronto: Some lessons for Australian cities. *Australian Planner* 29, 3: 149–154.

—, 1991b. Urban villages: Compact environements to help reduce major transport, economic, social and environmental problems in Australian cities. In *Forum on home: A place in the urban environment*. Proceedings of conference held on August 17–18. Sydney: University of Sydney Department of Architecture.

Kibble, Gabrielle, 1991. Metropolitan planning. In *Western Sydney's growth can we manage it? papers, summary of workshops and future strategies*. Blacktown: Western Sydney Regional Organisation of Councils.

Kinhill Engineers, 1989. *Rouse Hill urban release trunk drainage investigation*. Report prepared for the NSW Department of Planning. Sydney: Kinhill.

Kirwan, Richard, 1990. Infrastructure finance: Aims, attitudes and approaches. *Urban Policy and Research* 8, 4: 185–193.

—, 1991. *Financing urban infrastructure: Equity and efficiency considerations*. National Housing Strategy background paper number 4. Canberra: Australian Government Publishing Service.

—,1992. Urban form, energy and transport: A note on the Newman-Kenworthy thesis. *Urban Policy and Research* 10, 1: 6-23.

Klosterman, Richard, 1978. Foundations for normative planning. *Journal of the American Institute of Planners* 44: 37–46.

Krasniewicz, Louise, 1992. *Nuclear summer: The clash of communities at the Seneca women's peace encampment*. Ithaca: Cornell University Press.

Lang, Jill, 1990. The provision of social infrastructure in new urban development in three Australian states. *Urban Policy and Research* 8, 3: 91–104.

Levine, Ned, 1997. Credit distributed, new points raised. *Journal of the American Planning Association* 63, 2: 279–282.

Leyshon, Peter, 1992. Housing attitudes and consumer behaviour. Paper presented at the Royal Australian Institute of Architects national housing conference, housing for better urban environments, June, Canberra.

Logan, Bernard, 1992. Mini-city could house 250,000. *Sydney Morning Herald*, 21 February, 5.

Logan, John, and Harvey Molotch, 1987. *Urban fortunes: The political economy of place*. Berkeley: University of California Press.

Logan, P., and Luscombe, G.,1984. *Urban and rural capability study, North West Sector, Sydney*. Report prepared for the NSW Department of Environment and Planning. Sydney: Soil Conservation Service.

Lynch, Kevin, 1960. *The image of the city*. Cambridge, Massachusetts: MIT Press.

—, 1981. *A theory of good city form*. Cambridge, Massachusetts: MIT Press.

Lyotard, Jean Francois, 1984. *The postmodern condition: A report on knowledge*. Translated by G. Bennington and B. Massumi. Minneapolis: University of Minnesota Press.

MacIntyre, Alasdair, 1981. *After virtue: A study in moral theory*. London: Duckworth.

Macquarie Bank Limited, 1989. Rouse Hill Infrastructure Consortium: Presentation of water, sewerage and drainage cashflows. October. Prepared for Rouse Hill Infrastructure Consortium. Photocopy in author's files.

Majone, Giandomenico, 1989. *Evidence, argument and persuasion in the policy process*. New Haven: Yale University Press.

Mallett, William, 1993. Private government formation in the DC metropolitan area. *Growth and Change* 24: 385–415.

Mandelbaum, Seymour, 1990a. Reading plans. *Journal of the American Planning Association* 56: 350–356.

—, 1990b. Telling stories. *Journal of Planning Education and Research* 10, 3: 209–214.

—, 1997. Reading plans III. *Journal of Planning Education and Research* 16, 3: 230–232.

Manidis Roberts Consultants, 1991. *Proposed Rouse Hill Sewage Treatment Plant: Environmental impact statement*. Two volumes. Sydney: Rouse Hill Infrastructure Consortium.

Mannheim, Karl, 1952. *Essays on the sociology of knowledge*. Edited by Paul Kecskemti. London: Routledge and Kegan Paul.

Mansbridge, Jane, 1990. The rise and fall of self interest in the explanation of political life. In *Beyond self interest*. Edited by Jane Mansbridge. Chicago: University of Chicago Press.

Mant, John, 1992. *Inquiry into the Department of Housing*. Report. Available through the NSW Government Information Service, Sydney.

Marans, Robert, and Robert Zehner, 1974. Social planning and research in new communities. In *The contemporary new communities movement in the United States*. Edited by Gideon Golany and Daniel Walden. Urbana: University of Illinois Press.

Marcuse, Peter, 1989. Dual city: A muddy metaphor. *International Journal of Urban and Regional Research* 13, 1: 697–708.

Markus, R.A. 1967. Augustine and human action: Will and virtue. In *The Cambridge History of later Greek and early medieval philosophy*. Edited by A.H. Armstrong. Cambridge: Cambridge University Press.

Marris, Peter, 1987. *Meaning and action: Community planning and conceptions of change*. Revised edition. London: Routledge and Kegan Paul.

—, 1990. Witnesses, engineers, or storytellers? The influence of social research on social policy. In *Sociology in America*. Edited by Herbert Gans. Newberry Park, California: Sage.

—, 1996. *The politics of uncertainty: Attachment in private and public life*. London: Routledge.

Mascia-Lees, Frances, Patricia Sharpe, and Colleen Cohen, 1989. The postmodern turn in anthropology: Cautions from a feminist perspective. *Signs* 15, 1: 7–33.

Masterplan Consultants, 1987. *Monitoring the delivery of human services in new release areas. Main report, volume 1, delivery of services*. Blacktown: Western Sydney Regional Organisation of Councils.

McCloskey, Donald, 1985. *The rhetoric of economics*. Madison: University of Wisconsin Press.

—, 1990. *If you're so smart: The narrative of economic expertise*. Chicago: University of Chicago Press.

McDonald, Bruce, 1991. Introduction: Why the forum. In *Western Sydney's growth can we manage it? Papers, summary of workshops and future strategies*. Blacktown: Western Sydney Regional Organisation of Councils.

McGaw, Dickinson, 1991. Governing metaphors: The war on drugs. *American Journal of Semiotics* 8, 3: 57–74.

McLennan, W. 1996. *Year book Australia 1996*. Canberra: Australian Bureau of Statistics.

McLoughlin, Brian, 1992. *Shaping Melbourne's future: Town planning, the state and civil society*. Melbourne: Cambridge University Press.

McManus, Phil, 1992. Toronto – A model city? *Australian Urban Studies* 20, 3: 9–11.

Meinig, Donald, 1979. *The interpretation of ordinary landscapes: Geographical essays*. New York: Oxford University Press.

Metherell, Terry, 1991. Metherell: Why I defected. Resignation speech transcript. *Sydney Morning Herald*, 3 October, 4.

Meyer, Bob, 1990. Macarthur: Sydney's successful south western satellite. *Australian Planner* 28, 3: 25–30.

Meyerson, Martin, and Edward Banfield, 1955. *Politics, planning and the public interest: The case of public housing in Chicago*. New York: Free Press.

Miller, Donald, 1982. Metaphor, thinking and thought. *Etc.* 39, 2: 134–150.

Minnery, John, 1992. *Urban form and development strategies: Equity, environmental and economic implications*. National Housing Strategy background paper number 7. Canberra: Australian Government Publishing Service.

Minutes of the public meeting held on Sunday, 24 November 1991, at the Castle Hill Community Centre at 1.30 p.m called to consider North West Sector development. Photocopy. Copy in author's files.

Mitchell, R., and Rapkin, C. 1954. *Urban traffic: A function of land use*. New York: Columbia University Press.

Moore Milroy, Beth, 1989. Constructing and deconstructing plausibility. *Environment and Planning D* 7: 313–326.

—, 1991. Into postmodern weightlessness. *Journal of Planning Education and Research* 10, 3: 181–187.

Moore, Matthew, 1991. West to face big sewerage charges. *Sydney Morning Herald*, 1 July, 3.

Moriarty, Patrick, and Clive Beed, 1992. The end of the road for cars? *Urban Futures Journal* 2, 2: 10–14.

Morris, Raymond, 1984. Canada as a family. Ontario responses to the Quebec independence movement. *Canadian Review of Sociology and Anthropology* 21, 2: 181–201.

Munro-Clark, Margaret, and Ross Thorne, 1987. The democratization of planning: Some room for reform. *Australian Planner* 25: 27–33.

Murphy, Peter, and Ian Burnley, 1990. Regional issues affecting the financing of urban infrastructure in NSW. *Urban Policy and Research* 8, 4: 169–176.

Murphy, Peter, Ian Burnley, H. Harding, D. Weisner, and V. Young, 1990. *Impact of immigration on urban infrastructure.* Canberra: Australian Government Publishing Service.

Nash, June, 1989. *From tank town to high tech: The clash of community and industrial cycles.* Albany: State University of New York Press.

National Housing Strategy, 1991a. *Australian housing: The demographic, economic and social environement.* National Housing Strategy issues paper number 1. Canberra: Australian Government Publishing Service.

—, 1991b. *The affordability of Australian housing.* National Housing Strategy issues paper number 2. Canberra: Australian Government Publishing Service.

—, 1991c. *Financing Australian housing: The issues.* National Housing Strategy issues paper number 3. Canberra: Australian Government Publishing Service.

—, 1991d. *The efficient supply of affordable land and housing*: The urban challenge. National Housing Strategy issues paper number 4. Canberra: Australian Government Publishing Service.

—, 1992. *Housing location and access to services.* National Housing Strategy issues paper number 5. Canberra: Australian Government Publishing Service.

National Population Council Issues Committee, 1992. *Population issues and Australia's future: Environment, economy and society.* Final report. Canberra: Australian Government Publishing Service.

Nedeljkovic, Alex, 1991. Housing and urban planning private sector involvement in infrastructure provision case study. Sydney: Rouse Hill Infrastructure Consortium. Photocopy.

Neilson Associates, 1987. Net community benefits of urban consolidation. A report prepared for the City of Melbourne.

Nelson, John, Alan Megill, and Donald McCloskey eds, 1987. *The rhetoric of the human sciences: Language and argument in scholarship and public affairs.* Madison: University of Wisconsin Press.

Nesbitt, Heather, and Colin Donahee, 1990. Kellyville/Rouse Hill community Plan. A report prepared for Baulkham Hills Shire Council and the Department of Planning.

New South Wales, 1979. *Environmental planning and assessment act.* Number 203. Reprinted as at 2 April 1991. Sydney: NSW Government Printer.

—, 1990–91. *Parliamentary debates.* Third session of 49th parliament. Sydney.

—, 1992a. Submission by New South Wales Government to inquiry on taxation and financial policy impacts on urban setlements. Department of Local Government and Cooperatives section. Canberra: Industry Commission.

—, 1992b. Submission by New South Wales Government to inquiry on taxation and financial policy impacts on urban settlements. Water Board section. Canberra: Industry Commission.

—, 1992c. Submission by New South Wales Governement to inquiry on taxation and financial policy impacts on urban settlements. Cover letter. Canberra: Industry Commission.

Newman, Peter, 1990. The search for the good city. *Town and Country Planning* 59, 10: 272–275.

—, 1991. Presentation to meeting on "green transport". University of Technology, Sydney, September 5.

Newman, Peter, and Jeffrey Kenworthy, 1989a. *Cities and automobile dependence: A sourcebook.* Aldershot, England: Gower Technical.

—, 1989b. Gasoline consumption and cities: A comparison of US cities with a global survey. *Journal of the American Planning Association* 55, 1: 24–37.

—, 1991. *Towards a more sustainable Canberra.* Perth: Institute for Science and Technology Policy, Murdoch University.

—, 1992. *Winning back the cities.* Sydney: Pluto.

Newson, Janice, 1991. "Backlash" against feminism: A disempowering metaphor. *Resources for Feminist Research* 20, 304: 93–97.

Next Move Housing Ideas Competition, 1991. Competition packet. Part of home, a place in the urban environment: A project to explore new directions in higher density housing. Sydney: Departments of Architecture at the University of Sydney, University of Technology — Sydney, and the University of New South Wales.

Notes from the seminar with non-government welfare agencies, 1989. Seminar held at Youth Centre, Blacktown, September 19. Photocopy. Copy in author's files.

Orlans, Harold, 1953. *Utopia Ltd.: The story of the English new town of Stevenage.* New Haven: Yale University Press.

Osborn, Frederick, and Arnold Whittick, 1969. *The new towns: The answer to megalopolis.* London: Leonard Hill.

Parker, R.S., and P.N. Troy eds, 1972. *The politics of urban growth.* Canberra: Australian National University Press.

Payne, Martin, 1990. Implementation of urban development in Sydney: Recent experience and future issues. *Urban Policy and Research* 8, 4: 177–184.

Peattie, Lisa, 1991. Planning and the image of the city. *Places* 7, 2: 35–39.

—, 1987. *Planning: Rethinking Ciudad Guayana.* Ann Arbor, Michigan: University of Michigan Press.

Peel Mark, 1995. The urban debate: From "Los Angeles" to the urban village. In *Australian cities.* Edited by Patrick Troy. Melbourne: Cambridge University Press.

Percy, Walker, 1958. Metaphor as mistake. *The Sewanee Review* 66: 79–99.

Perin, Constance, 1977. *Everything in its place: Social order and land use in America.* Princeton: Princeton University Press.

—, 1988. *Belonging in America*: Reading between the lines. Madison: University of Wisconsin Press.

Phelan, Amanda, 1992. Moving out: The plans for Rouse Hill. *Northern Herald* supplement to the *Sydney Morning Herald*, 5 November, 1, 7.

Pincetl, Stephanie, 1992. The politics of growth control: Struggles in Pasadena, California. *Urban Geography* 13, 5: 450–467.

Powell, Diane, 1993. *Out west: Perceptions of Sydney's western suburbs.* Sydney: Allen and Unwin.

Pund, George, and Dick Fleming, 1997. Planning and delivering effective bus services in a new residential area. *Australian Planner* 34, 2: 78–82.

Pusey, Michael, 1991. *Economic rationalism in Canberra: A nation building state changes its mind.* Cambridge: Cambridge University Press.

Pynoos, Jon, 1986. *Breaking the rules: Bureaucracy and reform in public housing.* New York: Plenum Press.

Rainbow, Paul, 1989. *French modern: Norms and forms of the social environment.* Cambridge, Massachusetts: MIT Press.

Real Estate Research Corporation, 1974. *The costs of sprawl: Environmental and economic costs of alternative residential development patterns at the urban fringe, detailed costs analysis.* Washington, D.C.: United States Government Printing Office.

Richards, Lyn, 1990. *Nobody's home: Dreams and realities in a new suburb.* Melbourne: Oxford University Press.

Richardson, Jeremy, William Maloney, and Wolfgang Rudig, 1992. The dynamics of policy change: Lobbying and water privatization. *Public Administration* 70: 157–175.

Richmond, Jonathan. Forthcoming 1998. Simplicity and complexity in design for transportation systems and urban forms. *Journal of Planning Education and Research.*

Riddell, Adrienne, 1991. Group warns of area "Siberia". *Telegraph Mirror*, 15 July.

Roseth, John, 1992. Infrastructure pricing and urban settlement. *Australian Planner* 30, 3: 162–166.

Ross, Judith, 1989. The militarization of disease: Do we really want a war on AIDS? *Soundings* 72, 1: 39–58.

Rouse Hill Community Planning Team, 1989 to 1994. Minutes of meetings. Mount Druitt: Rouse Hill Community Planning Team (P.O. Box 46, Mount Druitt, NSW 2770).

—, 1992a. Report of public meeting held on October 18, 1992. Meeting held at Quaker's Hill Uniting Church, Sydney. Mount Druitt: Rouse Hill Community Planning Team (P.O. Box 46, Mount Druitt, NSW 2770).

—, 1992b. *Community services in Rouse Hill: What and when?* Issues papers, October. Mount Druitt: Rouse Hill Community Planning Team (P.O. Box 46, Mount Druitt, NSW 2770).

Rouse Hill Infrastructure Consortium, 1992 to 1994. *Rouse Hill Infrastructure Consortium News* 1, 2. (Rouse Hill Infrastructure Consortium, Mile End Road, Rouse Hill, NSW 2155).

—, 1993. *Rouse Hill Development Area and you.* Pamphlet. Rouse Hill: Rouse Hill Infrastructure Consortium (Mile End Road, Rouse Hill, NSW 2155).

Rydin, Y., and Myerson, G. 1989. Explaining and interpreting ideological effects: A rhetorical approach to greenbelts. *Environment and Planning D*, 7, 4: 463–479.

182   CONSTRUCTING SUBURBS

Sandercock, Leonie, 1990 (orig. 1975). *Property, politics and urban planning: A history of Australian city planning 1890–1990*. Second edition. New Brunswick, New Jersey: Transaction.
Sarat, Austin, and William Felstiner, 1986. Law and strategy in the divorce lawyer's office. *Law and Society Review* 20, 1: 93–134.
Sarkissian, Wendy, and Terry Doherty, 1987. *Living in public housing*. Red Hill, Australian Capital Territory: Royal Australian Institute of Architects.
Sahein, R., 1993. Representing urban America: 19th century views of landscape, space and power. *Environment and Planning D* 11, 1: 7–21.
Schneider, Mark, 1989. *The competitive city: The political economy of suburbia*. Pittsburgh: University of Pittsburgh Press.
Schon, Donald, and Martin Rein, 1994. *Frame reflection: Toward the resolution of intractable policy controversies*. New York: BasicBooks.
Schuman, H., and Scott, J., 1989. Generations and collective memories. *American Sociological Review* 54: 359–381.
Schwarz, Michiel, and Michael Thompson, 1990. *Divided we stand: Redefining politics, technology and social choice*. Philadelphia: University of Pennsylvania Press.
Searle, Glenn, 1984. Contribution of North West Sector to Sydney region urban development program. Internal report. Department of Environment and Planning Central Policy Division.
Shupe, Anson, and David Bromley, 1980. Walking a tightrope: Dilemmas of participant observation of groups in conflict. *Qualitative Sociology* 2, 3: 3–21.
Simmie, J.M., 1974. *Citizens in conflict: The sociology of town planning*. London: Hutchinson Educational.
Simons, P.L., and J.A. Black, 1992. *Transport and urban form for Australian cities: Final task force report*. Sydney: Australian Institute of Urban Studies NSW Division.
Sinclair Knight Buchanan, 1989a. *Rouse Hill Development Area public transport strategy*. Draft final report prepared for the NSW Department of Planning. Sydney.
—, 1989b. *Rouse Hill Development Area arterial and sub-arterial roads study*. Report prepared for the NSW Department of Planning. Sydney.
Smith, Jonathan, 1996. Geographical rhetoric: Modes and tropes of appeal. *Annals of the Association of American Geographers* 86, 1: 1–20.
Smith, Ruth, and Deborah Valenze, 1988. Mutuality and marginality: Liberal moral theory and working-class women in nineteenth-century England. *Signs* 13, 2: 277–298.
Soja, Edward, 1989. *Postmodern geographies: The reassertion of space in critical social theory*. London: Verso.
Southam, Kate, 1992. Community team plans services for Rouse Hill. *Northern Herald* supplement to the *Sydney Morning Herald*, 5 November, 7.
—, 1993a. Water Board admits pricing blunder. *Sydney Morning Herald*, 3 November, 4.
—, 1993b. Rouse Hill sewerage charges cut back. *Sydney Morning Herald*, 10 December, 6.
Spain, Daphne, 1993. Been-heres versus come-heres: Negotiating conflicting community identities. *Journal of the American Planning Association* 59, 2: 156–171.

Spearitt, Peter, and Christina DeMarco, 1988. *Planning Sydney's future*. North Sydney: Allen and Unwin with the Department of Planning.

Squires, Gregory ed, 1989. *Unequal partnerships: The political economy of urban redevelopment in postwar America*. New Brunswick: Rutgers University Press.

State Development, 1990. *Guidelines for private sector participation in infrastructure provision in the 'state of business'*. Sydney: State Development.

State Planning Authority, 1967. *Sydney region: Growth and change*. Sydney: State Planning Authority.

—, 1968. *Sydney region outline plan: 1970–2000 AD, a strategy for development*. Sydney: State Planning Authority.

State Pollution Control Commission and Water Board, 1985. *A strategy for the management of water quality of the Hawkesbury-Nepean River*. Sydney: State Pollution Control Commission.

Stein, Howard, 1990. In what systems do alcohol/chemical addictions make sense? Clinical ideologies and practices as cultural metaphors. *Social Science and Medicine* 30, 9: 987–1000.

Stein, Howard, and Robert Hill, 1977. The limits of ethnicity. *American Scholar* 46, 2: 181–189.

Stoker, Robert, 1987. Baltimore: The self-evaluating city? In *The politics of urban development*. Edited by Clarence Stone and Heywood Sanders. Lawrence, Kansas: University of Kansas Press.

Stretton, Hugh, 1974. *Housing and government*. Sydney: Australian Broadcasting Commission.

—, 1989 (orig. 1970) *Ideas for Australian cities*. Third edition, facsimile of 1975 text. Sydney: Transit Publishing.

Stubbs, J.G., and Barnett, J.R., 1992. Geographically uneven development of privatization: Towards a theoretical approach. *Environment and Planning A* 24: 112–135.

Swidler, Ann, and Jorge Arditi, 1994. The new sociology of knowledge. *Annual Review of Sociology* 20: 305–329.

Tauxe, Carolyne, 1995. Marginalizing public participation in local planning: An ethnographic account. *Journal of the American Planning Association* 61, 4: 471–481.

Tett, Alison, and Jeanne Wolfe, 1991. Discourse analysis and city plans. *Journal of Planning Education and Research* 10, 3: 195–200.

Thomas, Huw, and Patsy Healey eds, 1991. *Dilemmas of planning practice*. Aldershot, England: Avebury Technical.

Thorne, Ross ed, 1983. *Medium density housing in Sydney — 2 surveys: Attitudes of users and non-users*. Sydney: Ian Buchan Fell Research Centre, Department of Architecture, University of Sydney.

—, 1991. Housing as "home" in the Australian context. *PAPER: People and Physical Environment Research* 36, 5: 54–64.

Thorne, Ross, M. Diesner, Margaret Munro-Clark, and R. Hill, 1980. *Consumer survey of housing demand, sydney: 18–39 age group*. Sydney: Ian Buchan Fell Research project on Housing, University of Sydney.

Throgmorton, James, 1996. *Planning as persuasive storytelling: The rhetorical construction of Chicago's electric future*. Chicago: University of Chicago Press.

Throsby, David, 1991. *Ecologically sustainable development working groups: Urban issues intersectoral report.* Draft. Kingston, ACT: Ecologically Sustainable Development Secretariat.

Till, K., 1993. Neotraditional towns and urban villages: The cultural production of a geography of otherness. *Environment and Planning D* 11: 709–732.

Travers, Carmel, 1991. *City limits.* Television special, September 21. Sydney: Channel 7.

Trembath, Murray, 1991. Ban land releases. *Hills Mercury*, 16 July, 7.

Troy, Patrick, 1971. *Environmental quality in four Sydney suburban areas.* Canberra: Urban Research Unit, Research School of Social Sciences.

—, 1996. *The perils of urban consolidation.* Sydney: Federation Press.

Urban Development Committee, North West Sector Sub-Committee, 1983–1984. Minutes of meetings. Department of Planning.

Vipond, Joan, and S.K. Ho, 1992. The demographic dimensions of urban change. *Australian Planner* 30, 2: 81–85.

Water Board, 1985. *Baulkham Hills and Blacktown sewerage: Rouse Hill water pollution control plant – WPCP 31, stage 1 phases 1 and 2, technical data.* Sewerage planning and investigation 48/411, issued December 24. Sydney: Water Board.

—, 1990. *Blue green algae seminar. Proceedings, November 21–22.* Sydney: Water Board.

—, 1991a. *Improved effluent quality: Options of coastal sewage treatment plant upgrades, a public discussion document.* Sydney: Water Board.

—, 1991b. *Determining authority's report: Proposed Rouse Hill sewerage treatment plant.* Sydney: Water Board.

—, 1991c. Submission to House of Representatives standing committee for long term strategies inquiry on the pattern of urban settlement. Canberra: Commonwealth of Australia.

—, 1992. In Submission by New South Wales Government to inquiry on taxation and financial policy impacts on urban settlements. Canberra: Industry Commission.

Webster, Robert, 1991. The balance between employment, housing and the environment. In *Western Sydney's growth can we manage it? Papers, summary of workshops and future strategies.* Blacktown: Western Sydney Regional Organisation of Councils.

Westerman, Hans, 1991. Summing up and setting a programme for future action. In *Western Sydney's growth can we manage it? Papers, summary of workshops and future strategies.* Blacktown: Western Sydney Regional Organisation of Councils.

Western Sydney Regional Organisation of Councils, 1984. *Submission on the North-West Sector regional environmental study.* Blacktown: Western Sydney Regional Organisation of Councils.

—. No date. Fact sheet. Blacktown: Western Sydney Regional Organisation of Councils.

Williams, Bernard, 1985. *Ethics and the limits of philosophy.* Cambridge, Massachusetts: Harvard University Press.

Wilmoth, David, 1990. Urban infrastructure finance issues in Australia: A review in the context of international experience. *Urban Policy and Research* 8, 4: 159–168.

Wilson, Bob, 1990. Expansion of Sydney: Can the environment and the community afford It? Speech to the Urban Development Institute, 21 June 1990. Reprinted in *Developer's Digest* October: 20–24.

Windsor, Duane, 1979. A critique of the costs of sprawl. *Journal of the American Planning Association* 45, 3: 279–292.

Winston, Denis, 1957. *Sydney's great experiment: The progress of the Cumberland County plan.* Sydney: Angus and Robertson.

Wood, Gavin, and Shane Bushe-Jones, 1991. *Housing affordability: An international context.* National Housing Strategy background paper number 3. Canberra: Australian Government Publishing Service.

Woolcott Research, 1990. *Marketing strategy development study.* Three volumes. Report for the Green Street Joint Venture. Sydney: Woolcott Research.

Wozny, Lucy, 1989. The application of metaphor, analogy, and conceptual models in computer systems. *Interacting with Computers* 1, 3: 273–283.

Zannetides, Maria, 1991. Rouse Hill as an example of private sector involvement in the provision of infrastructure. Presentation notes for technical conference during visit by Tokyo Sewerage Bureau to Sydney Water Board, Sydney. October. Copy in author's files.

Zehner, Robert, 1977. *Indicators of the quality of life in new communities.* Cambridge, Massachusetts: Ballinger.

Zey, Mary, 1992. Criticisms of rational choice models. In *Decision making: Alternatives to rational choice models.* Edited by Mary Zey. Newbury Park, California: Sage.

Index

Economics
  economic men, 65
  economic rationalism, 52, 60
  language of debate, 60, 137
Elites
  bureaucratic, 7, 140
  business, 5, 7, 140
  political, 5
Environment. *See also* Bureaucrats; Planning, formal;
  Technical solutions
  environmentalists, 2
  generations and, 63
  impact assessment for Rouse
    Hill, 111–112
  natural, 54, 58, 159
  regulations, 47, 131
  standards and thresholds, 51,
    60
Environmental Planning and
  Assessment Act, 27, 35,
  98–102
Environmental services baselines,
  51
Equality. *See also* Fairness;
  Society; Urban form
  home ownership, 2
  spatial inequality, 57
  suburbs and, 42, 63
Ethics, 6, 20. *See also* Public
  interest
  incommensurability, 151
Expansionists, 42–47, 59, 61, 157
Experience and perspectives, 63–64
Experts
  manipulation and trust, 91–92
  role of, 80

Fairness, 47, 108
Families
  alternatives to nuclear, 57
  family life, 44, 56

generations, 63
nuclear, 45, 65
Federal government and urban
  issues, 31–34. *See also*
  Building Better Cities
Flint, Richard, 140. *See also*
  Department of Housing
Frameworks. *See* Perspectives
Freedom of Information Act and
  requests, 12, 129, 144, 156

Gender and generations, 63. *See
  also* Families
Generational effects, 62–63, 71,
  159
Goals, 158–159
Government. *See also* Federal
  government; Local govern-
  ment; State government
  Australian system, 22
Graphics. *See also* Aerial photo-
  graphs; Television
  Los Angeles/Toronto image,
    78
  map silences, 84
  Regional Environmental Plan,
    100–101
  slides as cues, 88
Great Britain planning, 4
Grounded theory, 14
Growth debates: *See* Urban form
Growth, population, 23–24. *See
  also* Immigration
Growth, urban, 9, 24. *See also*
  Urban development
  alternatives to, 3, 113–119
  environmental costs, 46
  social costs, 46
  suburban and fringe, 21, 48
  western Sydney, 23–24, 32, 48
Gyles Report, 139–140

public participation, 102
risk and, 130
Professionals, 7, 9, 66, 93
Property developer. *See* Developer
(role)
Public documents defined, 12
Public interest, 2, 5–7, 58,
159
critiques and disagreement 18
Department of Housing and, 140
ecological sustainability and,
153
powerful groups and, 5
public preferences and, 152–153
Public participation, 102–104
Pusey, Michael, 66

Quality of life, 60, 158
Quantification, 50–51, 60,
116–117, 137, 151

Rationality and reason, 2, 18,
150–154. *See also* Planning
process
Research
insider-outsider status, 12–13,
74
interviews, 10–12
methods described, 9–15
multiple sides and detachment,
13
Responsibility, 54, 156–158
Rhetoric
defined, 19
planning and, 2, 6
rhetorical devices, 5, 74, 91
Richards, Lyn, 66
Rouse Hill Community Planning
Team, 102, 123, 132–137
community and, 142–143
compared with consortium,
138–143

consolidationists and, 124
non-government groups, 133
Rouse Hill Development Area,
101. *See also* Planning,
formal
created, 97
Cumberland Plan and vicinity,
25
defining, 14
existing population, 84, 94–95
phasing and precincts,
126–128
uncertainty over population
demographics, 142–143
Rouse Hill Infrastructure Consortium, 31, 85, 123,
125–132, 138–141, 146. *See
also* Conspiracy theories;
Rouse Hill Community
Planning Team
Rouse Hill, the place, 25–26

Schipp, Joe, 132. *See also*
Department of Housing
Scientific environmentalists,
50–53, 61
Semiotics, 95
Sewage treatment
controversies, 109
Rouse Hill plant, 111–112
Simplification, evidence, 90
Social reform, 124
Social services. *See* Human
services
Society. *See also* Isolation, social.
destructive character, 65
diversity, 65
environmentalists' positions, 52
shared ideas, 154
social division, 57–58
social problems, 65–66
thin conception, 65

For Product Safety Concerns and Information please contact our EU
representative GPSR@taylorandfrancis.com
Taylor & Francis Verlag GmbH, Kaufingerstraße 24, 80331 München, Germany

* 9 7 8 9 0 5 7 0 0 5 2 7 5 *